How to overcome FEAR STRESS & ANGER

Tarit Kumar Pal

PUSTAK MAHAL®

Administrative office and sale centre

J-3/16 , Daryaganj, New Delhi-110002
☎ 23276539, 23272783, 23272784 • *Fax:* 011-23260518
E-mail: info@pustakmahal.com • *Website:* www.pustakmahal.com

Branches
Bengaluru: ☎ 080-22234025 • *Telefax:* 080-22240209
E-mail: pustak@airtelmail.in • pustak@sancharnet.in
Mumbai: ☎ 022-22010941, 022-22053387
E-mail: rapidex@bom5.vsnl.net.in
Patna: ☎ 0612-3294193 • *Telefax:* 0612-2302719
E-mail: rapidexptn@rediffmail.com

ISBN 978-81-223-1591-2

Edition : 2016

Printed at: Radha Offset, Delhi

'How to Overcome Fear, Stress & Anger'
is dedicated to my Gurudev late Subhas Chakraborty,
my father late Shri Hemendra Nath Pal,
my mother late Shrimati Shujala Pal
and my father in-law
late Shri Satyendra Kumar Dutta Choudhury.

Acknowledgement

I am deeply indebted to my wife Srimati Urmimala Pal. Without her constant support and encouragement, it would not be possible for me to put up my experience and thought process in the form of this book. I must also thank my daughter Dr. Tanusree Khandai and son-in-law Dr. Nishikanta Khandai, who had been constantly encouraging me during my work. My grandson Prodyot Khandai as usual has always been a positive push behind all my efforts during the entire period of compilation of this book.

"Most of the supporting sketches and figures that feature in the book are the work of Sri Satadru Banerjee, a student of the Kolkata Arts College. Based on the theme of the book he had suggested the cover page design which was given the final shape with some modifications by the publisher. The shades of darkness and horror in the front cover page depicts the negative potential of fear and anger when unattended or untamed; the shinning moon on the other hand represents the fact that when handled and managed with rational and logical approach, fear and anger have the potential to bring brightness in human life. Fear, stress and anger are all associated with the functions of the neurons of human brain. The leafless dry branches of the tree shown in the front cover page represent the basic 'dendrite structure' of brain neurons. I am thankful to Satadru Banerjee and the publisher for the cover page design."

Lastly, I shall be failing in my duty if I do not express my gratitude towards my brother-in-law Dr. Shubhomoy Dutta Choudhury and my senior colleague in ISP, Sail, Burnpur Sri Jayanta Bagchi who had been a constant source of encouragement to me in all my endeavours.

Suddenly, the officer's eyes widened as deep teeth marks appeared on the young girl's arms and shoulders. The girl screamed shrilly as rows of red welts and deep gashes appeared on her flesh. The police guard quickly helped Clarita out of the cell. They fled to the captain's office.

"This is something I know nothing about," the incredulous police captain announced. He looked at the marks on the young girl's arms. It was as if some invisible monster had gnawed on the girl's slim body. "Tell the mayor, the chief of police, and the medical examiner to get right down here," the captain informed a sergeant.

The chief of police and the mayor arrived immediately. They made a quick examination of Clarita's wounds, checked the young girl's story with the police reports, and waited for the medical examiner.

"It's probably a case of an epileptic seizure," the physician announced on arrival, examining Clarita's arms. "She probably inflicted these wounds upon herself."

The mayor frowned. He lifted the young girl's hair and pointed to the back of her neck. "Then, doctor, tell me how she bit herself on the back of the neck?"

As the bewildered physician continued his examination, officials questioned the young girl. "What is attacking you," inquired Mayor Arsenio Lacson.

"It looks like a man with a big black cape," sobbed Clarita. "He has bug eyes and is very, very ugly! When he comes after me, he has his fangs bared and ready to bite me."

The doctor carefully examined the indentations in the teenager's flesh. "They certainly look like teeth marks," he concluded. He also admitted Clarita was not under the influence of drugs or alcohol.

The chief of police assigned an officer to guard the young girl until morning. "Don't put her in a cell," the mayor suggested. "Keep her here in the front office."

Under the full glare of office lights, the bug-eyed monster did not reappear during the night. The following morning, Clarita was charged with vagrancy and taken to a municipal courtroom. Before her case could be called, the teenager was attacked again by the invisible monster. Astonished spectators in the courtroom watched with amazement as Clarita screamed from the agonising pain of invisible jaws that ripped at her flesh.

Dr. Mariana Lara, the medical examiner, rushed to her assistance. "It's absolutely not an epileptic fit," the physician informed the newsmen. "These are real teeth marks. As you saw yourselves, they are not self-inflicted."

The open-mouthed reporters served as astonished witnesses to the horrible attack. "You don't have to convince us, doc," said an elderly police reporter, crossing himself.

The doctor looked up at the reporter. "Perhaps this is a case for the clergy," Dr. Lara said. The mayor and the archbishop were summoned.

When the baffled mayor arrived in the courtroom, it was evident that Clarita's strange case was beyond the ministrations of medicine. "You poor child," the mayor said. The pitiful girl was now covered with scores of deep teeth prints. Her flesh was bruised, swollen, and discoloured. The mayor ordered for his official automobile. "We must get that child to the hospital," he said.

Dr. Lara agreed. The suffering girl was led to the mayor's automobile. As Mayor Lacson held Clarita's hand, deep teeth imprints suddenly appeared on the opposite side.

"The bloodthirsty fiend is trying to chew off her hand!" the mayor cried. The trio approached the automobile. "Driver, I want you to get us to the hospital in record time. Use the siren!"

One glance at Clarita, and the driver turned on the siren, threw the car in gear, and expertly manoeuvred the mayor's automobile through the thick Manila traffic. It was a hair-raising ride, punctuated by the tortured girl's screams of excruciating pain.

Strangely, the attacks from the 'bug-eyed monster' ended when Clarita was admitted to the hospital, where she quickly recovered her health. Although several years have passed, Clarita Villanueva has never again been visited by the invisible caped entity that bared its teeth and sank fangs into her flesh.

Dr. Lara told newsmen, "While the phenomena simply defies any rational explanation, I don't mind telling you that I was scared out of my wits."

Was this violent, flesh-tearing manifestation the product of a hysterical teenager's mind? Or are there entities that are attracted to certain people and feed upon their energy? The answers lie somewhere in the realm of the unknown.

10. A Detective Ghost

This strange story began on February 21, 1977, when the body of Teresita Basa was found by the police. The forty-eight-year-old woman was lying on the floor of her high-rise Chicago apartment, stabbed to death and partially burnt.

Like so many other hopeful immigrants, Basa had come to the United States from the Philippines seeking employment and a better quality of life. She had been working as a respiratory therapist at Edgewater Hospital, and the police didn't have a clue towards solving the crime. Their initial impression was that perhaps she had been killed by a boyfriend. The real solution to the case, however, would eventually come from Basa's ghost.

Dr. Jose Chua and his wife also worked at the hospital, though they hadn't been particularly close to Teresita. But one evening, while at home in Skokie, a small city just outside Chicago, Mrs. Chua unexpectedly entered a strange sort of trance. She got up and walked into the bedroom, where she lay down. Then a strange voice, speaking in Tagalog (a Philippine language) issued from her mouth: "I am Teresita Basa." After the strange voice accused a hospital orderly of the murder, Mrs. Chua emerged from the spell. But she suffered similar spells during the next several days, declaring in the murdered woman's voice that the orderly, a black youth named Allen Showery, had taken her jewellery and given her pearl cocktail ring to his girlfriend.

Dr. Chua, terrified by the claims, was left with no alternative but to contact the local police. His call was turned over to Joseph Stachula and Lee Epplen, two veteran detectives.

The detectives were naturally sceptical of Dr. Chua's story, but with no other leads in the case, decided to follow it up. When they met with the Chuas, they questioned them minutely about the deceased Teresita Basa's claims. They especially asked

A series of historical novels included *The Sorry Tale*, set in the first century, and the 19th century *Hope Trueblood*. Her most celebrated spirit novel, *Telka*, was set in medieval England and penned in the language of the day, an archaic style Curran never studied.

Patience could 'dictate' two or more novels simultaneously, shifting from one to another while never losing her train of thought. And Curran proved the perfect collaborator, dutifully recording Patience Worth's remarkable stories of days long gone by.

8. The Menacing Skulls

When Myles Phillipson, a magistrate, moved into his new house, Calgarth Hall, in the Lake District in northern England, he invited all his friends to a house-warming party. The party was in full swing when, suddenly, the guests heard Phillipson's wife scream. They found her on the staircase, staring at two grinning skulls.

Phillipson took the skulls and threw them out of the house, but during the night the skulls reappeared on the staircase. In the days that followed, Phillipson tried every means to get rid of the skulls, but no matter what he did, they always returned.

News of the menacing skulls spread quickly, and soon Phillipson found that his business was in financial trouble. Over the next few months, his wealth steadily diminished until he was left virtually penniless. Finally, Phillipson died, a broken man.

It turned out that the two skulls were those of a man and his wife who had previously owned Calgarth Hall. Phillipson had desired to own the property so much that he had had them executed for a crime they had not committed.

On the night of the magistrate's death, the skulls could be heard laughing throughout the house. They had had their revenge at last.

9. The Bug-eyed Monster

The 18-year-old girl twisted on the floor of the jail cell. "He's coming to bite me again!" Clarita screamed. "Help! The monster is coming after me!"

The policeman assigned to guard the young girl laughed at the hysterical outbursts of the distraught prisoner. He did not believe her fantastic tale about a bug-eyed monster in a black cape that was trying to chew her up. Clarita had been arrested on the streets of Manila after screaming for protection from the monster. Even on skid row, such bizarre behaviour attracted a crowd of bleary-eyed observers from the taverns.

"Best case of drug traffickers I've ever seen," commented a burly, big-bellyed bartender.

"I think she's a drug addict," commented a woman. Whatever her problems, the police arrested Clarita Villanueva and placed her in a jail cell. "Those bars are made of iron," said the cynical policeman, "the real monsters are in the streets."

"He's after me," Clarita croaked, flailing her arms at an invisible entity.

the couple if Teresita claimed that she was raped as well as murdered. No rape had actually taken place and the detectives asked this question to see if the couple would follow the spurious lead. But the Chuas didn't take the bait. The investigators were also impressed by how much the Chuas seemed to know about the murder.

"To this day," wrote Stachula some time later, "I'm not quite sure that I believe how the information was obtained. Nonetheless, everything [was] completely true."

Working with these clues, the Evanston police searched Showery's apartment and found Teresita's jewels. They even found her pearl cocktail ring in the possession of his girlfriend. When confronted with the evidence, Showery confessed to the murder and was later convicted of the crime. The case was officially closed in August, apparently solved by the ghost of Teresita.

11. A Date with Doom

Lord Thomas Lyttleton was in a surprisingly jovial mood as he sat down to breakfast with close friends at his home in Epsom, Surrey, on November 24, 1779. But his guests choked on their kidneys and kedgeree as he joked that he had been visited during the night by the ghost of a girl who had killed herself after he seduced and deserted her.

She said that in exactly three days, he would be dead.

Later that day, Lord Lyttleton made a magnificent speech in the House of Lords. He continued his roistering life in London society. He assured friends that he had never felt better and arranged to stay the following weekend with Peter Andrews, a Member of Parliament who lived in Dartford, Kent.

But on the third night, as the clock struck the eleventh hour, Lyttleton suddenly clutched at his side, collapsed and died in the arms of his valet.

At exactly that moment, Andrews woke up at Dartford to find Lyttleton standing beside his bed, wearing the dressing gown the MP had left out for him.

"It's all over with me, Andrews," said the figure. Andrews followed his friend, but found Lyttleton's room empty, the dressing gown still hanging on its hook. Next morning, he learnt of his friend's death.

12. A Ghostly Extrication

During the summer of 1965, Peter and Irene Nierman moored their barge near Tertogenbosch in Holland. One day, while Peter was ashore, their five-year-old son, Willem, fell into the water. Irene screamed, but there was nothing she could do to save the boy. Her husband was ashore and she was expecting another child. Some workmen heard her cries, but they were too far away to prevent the boy from drowning in the fast-

Prologue

People generally have an inherent tendency to be in their comfort zone which may be any place, situation, event, relationship or experience where they do not feel any threat. However, when gripped by fear or anger, they automatically get shifted from their comfort zone towards a zone of discomfort. It is generally observed that people operating from their zone of discomfort often fail to explore and capitalize on their full potential. Fear and anger therefore need to be clearly understood and appropriately dealt with.

Fear and anger are human emotions. Like any other emotion, they occur spontaneously without a person's free will. They are always triggered by stimuli which can either be

- internal or external
- real or imaginary

Irrespective of whether the stimuli are internal or external, real or imaginative, the human mind responds in the same way. This is because the mind cannot differentiate between a real and an imaginary stimulus. Fear and anger have the following common characteristics:

- They can grip a person at any place and at any hour of the day.
- They are 'neutral energy' with potential to yield either positive or negative results depending on how a person makes use of the 'energy' inherent to them.
- They have the potential to generate stress which in turn causes the human body to respond with enhanced energy in the form of 'fight or flight' response. On immediate basis, the 'fight or flight'

response helps a person to either fight or flee away from the stressors (fear or anger activating stimuli). However, if the 'response' continues for long or occurs frequently, it can adversely affect a person's health and thinking ability.

- If left unattended or uncontrolled, they can turn a person into their slaves with devastating results.

There are various techniques through which a person can cool down his mind and body from the 'aroused state' of 'flight or flight' response. It is only when the mind and body is brought into the state of homeostasis that a person is able to think rationally, make strategies and implement action plans to neutralize the possible adverse effects of fear and anger and make use of their potential positive signals (wherever there are opportunities). The first two chapters of the book concentrate on discussions on the following:

- Characteristics of human emotions in general
- How fear and anger activate the human stress mechanism
- Various parts of the human brain and the activities performed by each of them in the human stress development circuit
- The 'fight or flight response'
- How the aroused body out of stress can be brought back into the state of homeostasis through application of relaxation responses.

To deal effectively with fear and anger and keep them under control, apart from having a cool and balanced mind, a person needs to have lot of knowledge about their various aspects. In chapter three and chapter four respectively, the various faces of fear and anger are discussed with special reference to different:

- causes of the occurrence of fear and anger
- forms in which fear and anger appear
- roles played by fear and anger in human life
- techniques to be adapted to keep the negative effects of fear and anger at bay

History reveals that all great people who have conquered fear and anger and achieved success attest to the fact that they both are the products of the human mind. Preparation to effectively manage fear and anger therefore has to start in the mind first with the belief that it is possible to:

- utilize their energy in a positive way
- neutralize their possible negative potential

Tarit Kumar Pal.
(Author)
Retired Executive Director, SAIL, ISP, Burnpur,
Q. 71 East Riverview Cooperative Housing Society,
Baisnabghata Patli Township,
Patuli, Kolkata 700094.
Mobile: 09832179193

Contents

Chapter Four : Anger & Its Different Faces

Chapter One

FEAR, STRESS & ANGER

Fear and anger are normal human emotions. While fear is induced by a threat perception, anger often floats on the base of fear. By nature both

- *are 'neutral energy' with potential to produce either positive or negative results depending on how people use them.*
- *have the potential to activate the stress mechanism which is inbuilt in the human DNA.*

Various parts of the brain are involved in the functioning of the human stress mechanism; they carry out specific activities in an organized manner. Stress causes physiological responses in the human body which in common parlance is known as 'Fight or Flight' response.

On immediate measure, this response aids people to get prepared with enhanced energy to either fight or flee away from the fear or anger perception. If this response however continues for long stretch of time or occurs frequently, it has the potential to affect people in the form of ill health and impaired mental faculty. In the current chapter, for general awareness, the following have been discussed:

- *Basic understanding of the human emotions*
- *How fear and anger set the stress mechanism into action and how different parts of the brain participate in it to cause the physiological response known as 'Fight or Flight' response*
- *Role of autonomic nerves and medulla glands in stress circuit*

To effectively deal with fear and anger, familiarization with the symptoms of the 'Fight or Flight' response, its merits and demerits and various techniques to cool down the aroused state of mind to a state of homeostasis are very important. These are all discussed in chapter two.

1. HUMAN EMOTIONS

A person experiences some kind of an emotion all the time; in fact, he goes through different emotional states throughout the day, sometimes even without his awareness. Human emotions are always triggered by stimuli and occur spontaneously without a person's free will. Irrespective of whether the stimulus triggering a particular emotion is real or imaginative, the mind responds the same way. This is because the human mind cannot differentiate between real and imaginary stimulus.

An emotion is always perceived. A perception can be described as a human trait that enables a person to become aware of something through his five organs of senses. It is formed out of observation, interpretation or mental image that a person holds with regard to events, conditions or circumstances.

Since perception is opinion based, it is directly linked to a person's thought.

Thought is the origin of human emotion. A thought is produced when an external stimulus enters the mind through the five senses i.e. seeing, smelling, tasting, hearing and touching; it causes a wide range of human feelings known as 'affect'. Affect is experienced by people in the form of either emotion or mood. Though they are closely related, there are differences between 'emotion' and 'mood' as mentioned below. An emotion:

- is caused by specific event but the cause of a mood is often general and unclear.
- generally lasts for short duration. The lasting duration of the mood on the other hand is longer compared to emotion.

- is specific and numerous in nature like anger, fear, joy, sadness etc. But mood is general and has two dimensions – positive and negative which may comprise of multiple specific emotions.
- is usually accompanied by facial expressions, but a mood does not necessarily have any indication of expressions.
- is action oriented by nature but a mood is cognitive in nature.

Every situation in life that produces an emotional reaction has two basic components.

- The situation itself
- The reaction to the situation

Emotions have strong link with human memories. It is a common knowledge that even when a situation is over, its reaction part continues to live in the memory in the subconscious mind of the concerned person. Memories are not just facts which are stored in the subconscious mind; they are very much associated with the emotions people felt at those times when the facts occurred. That is why if a person thinks of an unhappy incident of the past, he starts feeling unhappy again. Similarly, if a person thinks of a happy incident of the past, he starts feeling happy while recollecting the event in the mental picture.

2. EMOTIONAL RESPONSES

All emotional responses have the following components of expressions:

- Subjective.
- Physiological.
- Expressive.

Subjective component refers to the way a person experiences his feelings. Generally, a person's emotion cannot be measured by others. Unless the person experiencing the emotion describes his feelings, others cannot know about it in totality. Description and interpretation of feelings even under similar circumstances can vary from person to person. The experiences of emotions can be of pleasure as well as of displeasure. Emotions are always person specific. The same circumstance may be pleasurable for one person and boring for another and the intensity of feelings also varies from person to person.

Physiological responses of emotions such as increase in heart beat, blood pressure etc. can be scientifically measured. Although the psychological response of each emotion is different, there are several different emotions which produce similar physiological responses, for example, fear and anger both produce similar physiological responses known as the 'Fight or Flight' response. Fight or Flight is the physiological response against the stress developed out of a fearful event or an emotional attack from anger.

Expressive component is the outward expression of a person's emotional feelings. It embraces various forms of facial/bodily expressions like flushed face, tensing of muscles, tone of the voice, rapid breathing, restlessness, gestures, attitude etc. From the outward expressions, people in general develop a learning to read and figure out the feelings of a person they are closely associated with. Though this often forms the basis on which social interactions are regulated, it does not necessarily reveal the feelings of the person in totality under all circumstances. Past experience and cultural backgrounds also play important role in the translation and determination of the outward expressions of a person's feelings. While in some culture, a person avoiding looking directly at a person in authority signifies respect, in other cultures it may be considered as an expression of guilt or trustworthiness.

Each of the emotions is expressed in terms of varying degrees of intensity like mild, moderate and strong. For example,

- Anger in a mild form is expressed as disgust or dismay, at a moderate level is expressed as offended or exasperated and at an intense level is expressed as rage or hate.
- Joy in a mild form is expressed as delight, at a moderate level is expressed as jubilation and at an intense level is expressed as ecstasy.

Emotions are not specific to any person. In fact the same person may also go through different emotions at different periods of time and behave differently. When a person is in emotional state of apathy, he generally:

- becomes careless towards others
- talks very little or nothing
- has strong doubt of own reality
- is persistent towards self-destruction, thinks about suicide, cries for pity, shows very little ability for solving problems of survival and is very close to his own demise

When the person is in the emotional state of anger, he generally:

- is blatant and destructive
- is unreasonable and can't be trusted
- has brutal sense of humour and often takes the 'I am right – you are wrong stand'
- uses alarming lies.

When the person is in the emotional state of enthusiasm, he generally:

- shows intense interest in life, has an inherent sense of responsibility and can be trusted
- feels high self-worth and respects others and finds existence full of pleasure
- communicates well and accepts exchange of beliefs and ideas to broaden own reality
- is highly creative and persistent with action, has elevated reasoning capacity and is very fast in responding.

☙❧

3. EMOTION IS ENERGY

All emotions basically are "neutral energy". However depending on how they are being dealt with, they have the potential to yield either positive or negative outcome. The word emotion is derived from the latin word 'emotere' which means energy in motion. In the state of any emotion, what a person generally senses, is the experience of energy moving through his body that creates vibrations of particular frequency.

It is a common knowledge that sound has energy, and that energy takes the form of a wave. Like sound, emotion also takes the form of a wave and is characterized by wave parameters. Various parameters related to emotional waves are discussed in the subsequent paragraphs.

Figure no. 1 represents a wave cycle drawn against time that demonstrates various parameters of a normal wave cycle. The amplitude of a wave is the distance from the centre line or the still position to the top of a crest or to the bottom of a trough. In a wave, amplitude determines the amount of energy which is being transported by the wave. The larger the amplitude, the more energy a wave has. A *wave frequency* is the number of cycles or oscillations that are completed in a certain amount of time. It is generally expressed in per second. *Wavelength* is the distance between two successive crests or troughs of a wave.

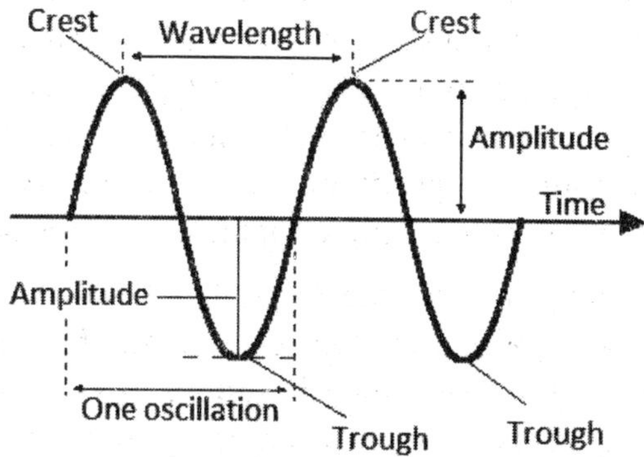

Crest
Wavelength
Crest
Amplitude
Time
Amplitude
One oscillation
Trough
Trough
Frequency = Number of oscillations per seconds

Figure no. 1

Each emotion has its own vibratory signature. On the basis of the amount of energy associated with them, emotions are broadly classified into following two categories:

Low energy emotion (refer figure no. 2).

High energy emotion (refer figure no. 2).

High energy emotion has high frequency, high amplitude and shorter wavelength
Low energy emotion has low frequency,low amplitude and higher wavelength
Low energy emotional wave
High energy emotional wave
Amplitude is directly related to the energy an emotional wave transports

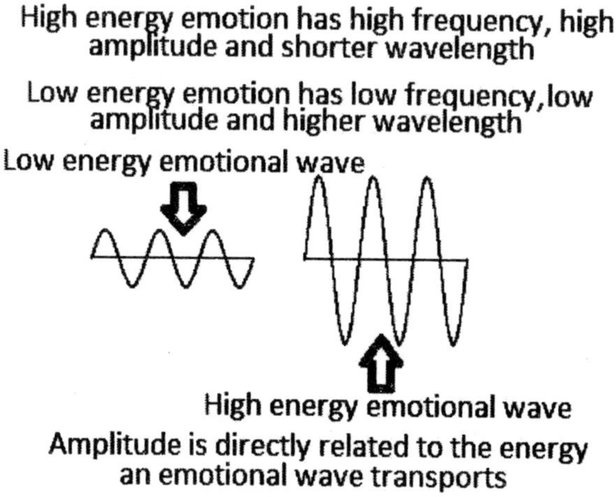

Figure no. 2

High energy emotions resonate at high frequency, high amplitude and short wavelength. They generally make people feel better, more active, and more uplifted; this is because their energy is higher and circulating at a much higher frequency. Happiness, elation, joy, gratitude, appreciation, compassion, love etc. are some of the examples of high energy emotions.

Low energy emotions on the other hand resonate at low frequency, low amplitude and long wavelength. They generally make people feel worse, sluggish and depressed with slow moving energy. This is because emotions with low energy permeate human being with a slow moving and lowered energy state. Sadness, worry, anger, irritation, fear, frustration, rage etc. are some of the examples of low energy emotions.

4. FEAR & ANGER ACTIVATE STRESS

It has been mentioned earlier that while fear is induced by a threat perception, anger often floats on the base of fear. Both have the potential to generate stress through the activation of the stress mechanism which is inbuilt in human DNA. The triggering impulse (i.e. the stimulus activating fear or anger) that sets the stress mechanism into action is known as stressor.

On activation, the stress mechanism sets different parts of the brain into action. This leads to series of actions within the body that finally culminate into various physiological responses. For ease of understanding of how the stressor sets the stress mechanism into action and how the human body reacts to it subsequently, the following need to be clearly understood.

- Roles played by different parts of the brain that takes part in the stress phenomenon.
- Different routes through which stress mechanism works.
- How human nervous system reacts to stress mechanism.
- How medulla gland system reacts to the nervous system.
- The physiological responses against stress.

Human brain is a complex organ; it comprises of an intricate network of communications which form the starting point of everything a person senses, thinks or does. The cells in the human brain are constantly transferring information and triggering responses. Some of these communications produce conscious thoughts and actions while others produce autonomic responses. Amongst the various parts of the human brain, there is a small portion called the limbic system. The limbic system comprises of nerves and networks spread over several areas; it controls the basic emotions like fear, anger etc. It is also known as emotional brain. Different parts of the brain that participate in the stress mechanism circuit are:

- sensory thalamus
- sensory cortex
- hippocampus
- amygdale (plural of amygdala)
- hypothalamus

Sensory thalamus sits on the top of the brain stem and is composed of two symmetrical parts often referred as lobes. Basically it receives impulse from the stimulus (stressor) and transmits it forward. On receipt of signal from the stressor, the sensory thalamus transmits the signal to amygdale through two different routes. Both the routes of communication work simultaneously but generate responses with split second difference in time. The responses from both the routes may or may not match with each other, but on all occasions the response of the body through the longer route (which utilizes the thinking capacity of the mind) eventually prevails.

The sensory cortex embraces parts of the brain that receive the impulse from the sensory thalamus and reads it for interpretation. It processes and makes sense out of information gathered through the five human senses – vision, audition (sound), olfaction (smell), gestation (taste) and somatosensation (touch). Each sense has its own area of primary sensory cortex. Primary cortex sends information to the secondary sensory cortex (also known as unimodal association cortex) for further processing. If the secondary sensory cortex detects and establishes context, it sends the message to amygdale, but if it fails to produce response, multimodal association cortex comes into effect for further processing and integration of multiple senses. If the multimodal association cortex establishes context, it sends the message to amygdale or else it sends the information to hippocampus for further processing in order to establish context.

The hippocampus is a horseshoe-shaped structure. There is one hippocampus in each of the hemispheres of the brain. Hippocampus stores memories and can retrieve them later. It receives affective impulses from sensory cortex, integrates those with stored memories by applying logic to generate meaningful information and passes it on to amygdale.

Amygdale is the plural of amygdala. Each hemisphere has one amygdala. The amygdale is responsible for the final assessment of whether the stressor is a threat or otherwise. It has the capacity to store memories of events and emotions which can be recognized and related to in future. The amygdale eventually relay the processed final message to the hypothalamus.

Hypothalamus is a region of the brain, between the thalamus and the mid brain. It functions as the main control center for the autonomic nervous system. If the hypothalamus receives threat (arising out of fear/anger) signal from the amygdale, it immediately activates the sympathetic nervous system of the autonomic nervous system which in turn activates the adrenal medulla gland system. If on the other hand, the hypothalamus receives 'no threat' signal from the amygdale, it then activates the parasympathetic nervous system of the autonomic nervous system. Parasympathetic nervous system acts directly against sympathetic nervous system.

ঙ্গষ্ঠ

5. STRESS ACTIVATION ROUTES

Irrespective of whether the stressors are real or imaginative, they stimulate and activate the human stress mechanism the same way. The impulse of the stressor is forwarded simultaneously through the following two separate routes of communications in the brain:

- Route no. 1
- Route no. 2

Route no. 1 (shown in figure no. 3): On receipt of the threat signal from the stressor, the sensory thalamus in this route passes the information directly to the amygdale which in turn passes the information to the hypothalamus. On getting the threat signal, the hypothalamus immediately activates the sympathetic nervous system. The sympathetic nervous system then automatically sets the adrenal medulla gland system into operation. The sympathetic nervous system works through the nerves and the adrenal medulla gland system works through the blood stream. The combined effect of the above two systems brings about physiological changes which energizes the body of a person and makes him ready to either face the threat perception or flee away from it. This physiological response of the body of a person is known as fight or flight response. In this route the stress mechanism completes its functions even before the thinking part of the brain processes or evaluates what really is happening.

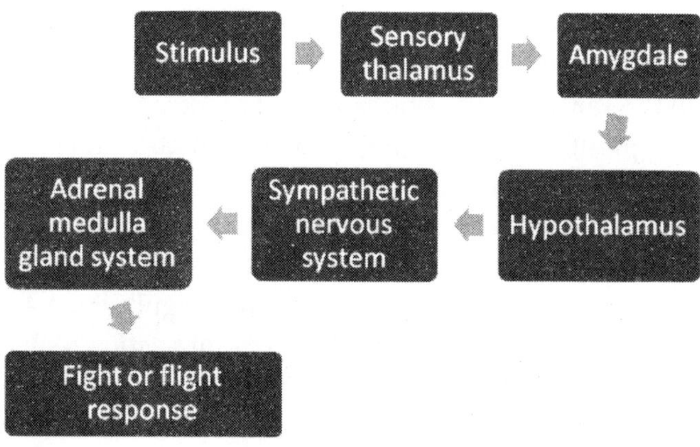

Figure no. 3

Route no. 2 (shown in figure no. 4): In this route, the thinking part of the brain becomes active. The sensory thalamus, on receiving the threat signal relays the message to the sensory cortex, instead of directly sending it to amygdale (as in the case of route no. 1). The sensory cortex on receipt of the information applies its discriminatory faculty to assess the information received. As mentioned earlier, the sensory cortex functions through primary sensory cortex, unimodal association cortex and multimodal (also known as polymodal) association cortex. Generally:

- when the stressor is an object, the unimodal association cortex is able to establish context and send its findings to amygdale.
- when the stressor is a concept, the polymodal association cortex is able to establish context and sends its findings to amygdale.

When the primary sensory cortex, the unimodal sensory cortex and the polymodal association cortex are unable to integrate the received information, the information automatically is passed on to the hippocampus to establish the context. After processing, the hippocampus relays its findings to amygdale. If the amygdale receive messages from any of the sensory cortex or from the hippocampus which rule out the possibility of any impending threat, the information is relayed to the hypothalamus. The hypothalamus in such a case immediately activates the parasympathetic nervous system to bring the already aroused body (aroused through the action of the route no. 1) to a state of homeostasis (figure no. 4 A). The parasympathetic nervous system comes into action only when the amygdale give the no threat signal to the hypothalamus and works directly against the action of sympathetic nervous system.

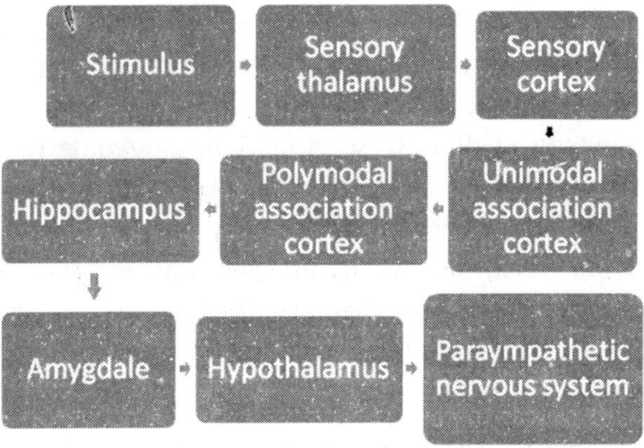

Figure no. 4 A

In the second route, if the impulse of the stressor on reaching amygdale after passing through sensory thalamus, sensory cortex/unimodal association cortex/polymodal association cortex/hippocampus is considered to be a threat, it will not create any shock to the person as his body is already in a state of arousal through the action of route no. 1 which acted a split second earlier. In this case the Fight or Flight response will remain active through the actions of the sympathetic nervous system and adrenal medulla gland system (figure no 4 B).

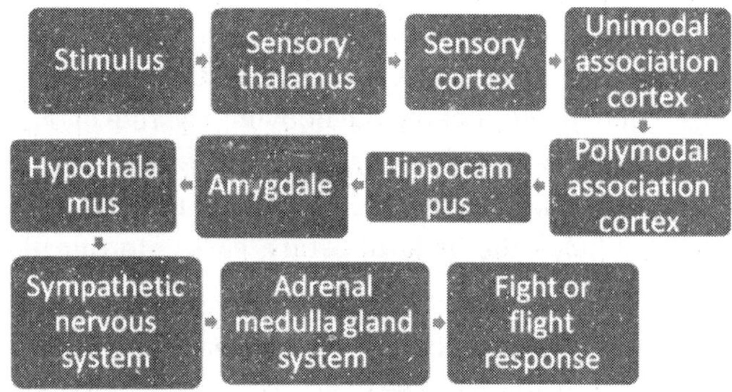

Figure no. 4 B

When a person is deeply engrossed in reading a book in a library and a book- shelf collapses, on hearing the sudden and unexpected sound of the shelf collapsing, he often gets scared. This is because on hearing the sudden and loud noise, the fear perception (stressor) instantly sets the brain into action which in turn immediately activates the stress mechanism through route no. 1. Amygdale in this case relay threat perception to hypothalamus which activates the sympathetic nervous system. Sympathetic nervous system in turn activates the medulla gland system. The combined action of the above two systems cause the 'Fight or Flight response'.

Split seconds after the route no. 1 functions, when the thinking part of the brain becomes active, if the brain collects enough information to realize that there is no impending danger and that the noise in fact was the sound of a book-shelf collapsing, it then turns off the fear reaction. Here, the amygdale send no threat signal to the hypothalamus which in turn activates the parasympathetic nervous system. All these happen in seconds. In this case, route no. 2 is active. Route no. 2 always nullifies the effects of route no. 1 and prevails over it.

It implies from above that when the amygdale convey threat signal to the hypothalamus, it activates the sympathetic nervous system which in turn activates the medulla gland systems. They together carry the body into a state of 'Fight or Flight' response. When the amygdale convey no threat signal to the hypothalamus, it activates the parasympathetic nervous system. This helps the body to return back into the state of homeostasis.

The functions of the following two systems involved in the 'Fight or Flight' response have been discussed in details in the subsequent sections.

- Sympathetic and parasympathetic nervous systems of human autonomic nervous system.
- Adrenal medulla gland systems.

6. HUMAN NERVOUS SYSTEM

Stress mechanism activated by fear or anger is directly connected to the human autonomic nervous systems. To know how the autonomic nervous system works, familiarization with the human nervous systems is very important. Human nervous systems have the following two major components:

(I) The central nervous system (CNS), comprising of the nerves in the brain and the spinal cord area and

(II) The peripheral nervous system (PNS), comprised of all the other nerves (other than CNS) in the body.

The peripheral nervous system again has two basic components:

- Somatic nervous system (SNS),
- Autonomic nervous system (ANS).

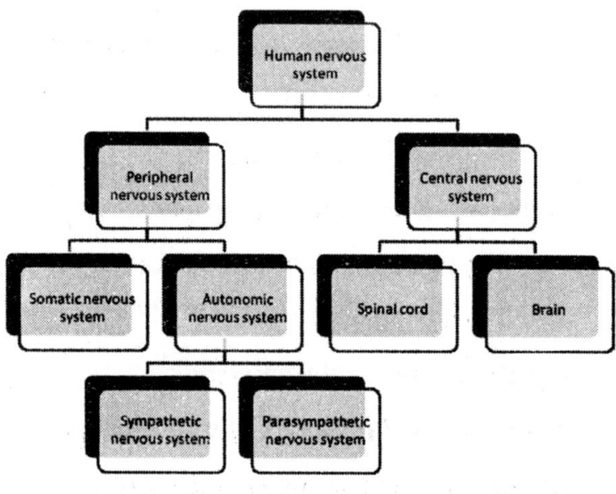

Figure no. 5

The somatic nervous system is made up of nerves that are connected to skin, muscles and sensory organs (the eyes, ears, nose, skin, etc.). It is responsible for voluntary control of muscles, as well as reception of sights, sounds, sensations, tastes and smells. In movement, the somatic nervous system carries impulses from the brain (CNS) to the muscle to be moved, while in its sensory capacity, the somatic nervous system carries impulses from the sensory organ to the brain (CNS).

Autonomic nervous system which functions involuntarily has two components:

- Sympathetic nervous system.
- Parasympathetic nervous system.

Activation of the sympathetic nervous system

- dilates the pupils
- opens the eyelids
- stimulates the sweat glands
- dilates the blood vessels in large muscles
- constricts the blood vessels in the rest of the body
- increases the heart rate
- opens up the bronchial tubes of the lungs
- inhibits the secretions in the digestive system

When activated, the parasympathetic nervous system cause

- pupil constriction
- activation of the salivary glands
- stimulation of the secretions in the stomach
- stimulation of the activity of the intestines

- stimulation of secretions in the lungs
- constriction of the bronchial tubes
- decrease in heart rate
- conservation of energy

When the hypothalamus in the brain receives a threat signal, the sympathetic nervous system is automatically activated which in turn activates the adrenal medulla gland system.

7. ADRENAL MEDULLA GLANDS

It has been mentioned earlier that on receipt of threat signal from amygdale (arising out of fear or anger), the hypothalamus immediately activates the sympathetic nervous system. This in turn automatically activates the medulla gland system.

Adrenal gland system consists of two triangular shaped organs located at the top of each kidney. Each of them has two parts with distinct functions (refer figure no. 6).

(I) Adrenal cortex (the outer part of the gland).

(II) Adrenal medulla (the inner part of the gland).

Adrenal cortex has three concentric regions namely, outer, middle and inner. Each region produces its own set of hormones. Hormones basically are chemical substances produced at one site which initiates or regulates the activity of an organ or group of cells in another part of the body. The adrenal cortex secretes a number of steroid hormones. These steroids are broadly classified into the following three groups (refer figure no. 6):

- **Mineralocorticoids:** These hormones stimulate absorption of sodium by the kidneys and regulate the water and salt balance in the body. Aldosterone is an important mineralocortoid.
- **Glucocorticoids:** These hormones are responsible for regulating the process of metabolism of carbohydrates, proteins and fats. The most important amongst the glucocorticoid hormone is cortisol.

- **Gonadocorticoids:** These are sex regulating hormones. They are involved in creating and maintaining the differences between men and women.

Death would result if the adrenal cortex stops functioning as it controls important metabolic processes essential to life. The hormones released by adrenal medulla glands, however are not directly involved in the living of a person, but they do play important role in helping him to deal with physical and emotional stress. The following hormones of the adrenal medulla glands are released directly into the blood stream after the sympathetic nervous system is stimulated:

- Epinephrine
- Norepinephrine

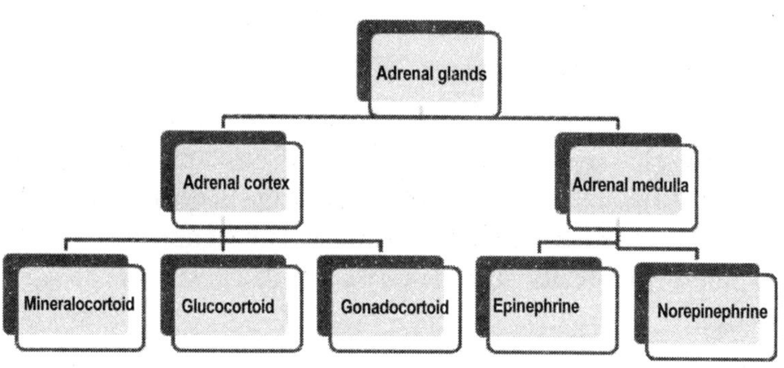

Figure No. 6

In actions, though epinephrine and norepinephrine apparently appear to be similar, they differ from each other in many of their effects. While norepinephrine constricts almost all blood vessels, the epinephrine causes constriction in some of the networks of minute blood vessels only but dilates the blood vessels in the skeletal muscles and the liver. Both hormones increase the rate and force of contraction of the heart. This increases the output of blood from the heart with increase in blood pressure. Epinephrine stimulates the breakdown of glycogen which is the liver's storage form of glucose and triggers the release of blood sugar.

Both hormones increase the level of circulating free fatty acids. The extra amounts of glucose and fatty acids which flood into the blood stream, supply energy to all parts of the body. This energy is used by the body during perceived stress out of fear or anger when increased alertness is required. Epinephrine is sometimes called the 'emergency hormone' because it is released during stress and its stimulatory effects fortify and prepare a person to either fight with the stressor or flee away from it. However it is noted that persistent surge of epinephrine can damage blood vessels, increase blood pressure and raise risk of heart attacks and brain strokes while norepinephrine can lead to vasoconstriction i.e. the narrowing of blood vessels. This results in high blood pressure.

It has already been discussed that the dual actions of sympathetic nervous system and adrenal medulla gland systems bring about a physiological change in the human body in the form of Fight or Flight response. The significance of this response, its merits and demerits are discussed in the next chapter.

Chapter Two

STRESS RELIEVING

How stress generated out of fear and anger causes Fight or Flight response has been discussed in chapter one. Awareness of the symptoms associated with Fight or Flight response is very important. This is because, many times fear and anger run their courses even before a person understands anything. 'Awareness' therefore serves as a guide to make the person understand that he is under an attack from fear or anger; this in turn enables him to initiate appropriate action plans to bring the stressed and aroused state of mind back to normal state.

Fight or Flight response is life saving in emergency situation and helps a person to either fight with or flee away from the stimuli creating the fear or anger perception. Repeated bouts of Fight or Flight response or its occurrences for longer can have severe adverse effects on a person's mind-body complex. On a long term basis, Fight or Flight response has the potential to cause a person various health hazards and impairment of his thinking ability which has direct impact on his/her decision making.

Therefore, stressful situations caused either by fear or anger need to be addressed and handled very carefully. Application of various techniques through which aroused states of mind can be calmed down and brought to the states of homeostasis can broadly be clubbed into the following categories:

- Muscular relaxation
- Relaxation through breathing
- Relaxation through meditation

Once the mind body complex is brought to the state of homeostasis, various aspects of fear and anger can be analyzed and decisions taken to effectively deal with them in order to manage them appropriately.

8. FIGHT OR FLIGHT RESPONSE

As discussed in chapter one that as soon as a person undergoes stress out of fear or anger, within split seconds certain physiological changes take place in his body through the automatic and dual actions of autonomic nervous system which works through the nerve path and adrenal medulla gland systems which works through the blood stream. This response of the body under stress is known as Fight or Flight response. Some of the physiological changes associated with Fight or Flight response are mentioned below:

- The level of circulating free fatty acid in the blood is increased along with increase in the blood sugar. Together they supply extra energy to the body through the blood stream.
- Some of the less important minute blood vessels get constricted while many of the important blood vessels get dilated. Blood is diverted from stomach towards skeletal muscles to supply them extra energy; this causes tightening of the stomach muscles with adverse affect on the digestive system. Blood is also diverted from the skin to the more important areas as the peripheral blood vessels get constricted.
- Blood circulation improves with increased heart beat rate. This helps in increased blood circulation to some of the vital parts of the body that require extra energy during that period. Rapid heart rate in response to stress caused by fear or anger often makes a person feel that his heart is going

to explode. This is mainly because of the fact that the heart during this period works diligently to provide as much blood as possible to the body to deal with the perceived threat. It is said that the amount of blood pumped by the heart increases fivefold during the Fight or Flight response.

- Increase in breathing rate associated with widening of bronchial passageway of air from the nasal/oral cavity to the lungs enable the body to draw additional air from the atmosphere to ensure additional energy availability in the form of oxygen.
- Perception of pain diminishes with intensification of awareness and reflex action.
- Blood develops the tendency to clot quicker. This reduces the risk of blood loss in case of any injury during this period.
- The pupils of the eyes get dilated with attended sharpness of sight.
- Increase in body sweating enables the skin to experience a cooling effect. Saliva gland secretion reduction causes drying up of mouth.
- Activities of immune system get temporarily withdrawn.

All the above changes provide additional energy to a person that enables him to withstand the sudden shock from the effect of stress and get prepared to either directly face the stressful situation or flee away from it. Because the physiological responses mentioned above help a person to prepare to fight or flee away from the stressor, they are known as Fight or Flight response.

ଓଃଧ

9. RELAXATION RESPONSE

Fight or Flight response auto works against stress and is inbuilt in human DNA. It is life saving in emergency situation. However, if it persists for long or is frequently activated by the stress of everyday life, it can make a person down and lead him towards various physical ailments in the form of problem with

- cardiovascular systems
- muscles and joints
- body's immune systems
- endocrine systems
- respiratory systems
- skins
- gastro-intestinal system and so forth.

The stress by its nature bypasses the rational mind where more thought out beliefs exist and normally takes a person into an attacking mode. Also it makes one's thinking process distorted. This often causes him to look negatively at the world around him.

In view of the above, it is essential that whenever the mind is aroused, it is immediately brought back from the state of arousal to a state of homeostasis. Once it is done, a person will be in a better frame of mind to introspect and evolve specific strategies to effectively deal with a fear/anger perception.

To calm down the mind from aroused state of stress, there are numbers of identified relaxation techniques. These are all mentally active processes which can broadly be clubbed into three groups.

- Muscular relaxation
- Relaxation through breathing.
- Relaxation through meditation.

However there is no single relaxation technique which is considered to be the best for everybody. The choice of the practice/practices to be adapted depends on a number of factors like a person's specific needs, preferences and fitness level etc.

The choice of relaxation technique also depends on the way a person intends to react to stress arising out of fear/anger. If felt appropriate, a person can alternate or even combine different techniques to get the best result for him. To get better results, the techniques should not be applied only when a person is under the clutch of stress, they should fit into his daily routine just like brushing of teeth. Relaxation techniques are skills which need to be developed through practice, practice and practice.

Apart from the relaxation techniques mentioned above, cold water treatment is also an efficient method of stress relieving. Cold water treatment in the form of shower bath helps is quick cooling of the mind and body. Water aids in distribution of prana (vital energy) throughout the body and brings in freshness.

Spinal bath is also a very effective treatment for soothing frayed and tense nerves. Spinal bath is a technique in which the spine is soaked in an approximately five centimeter thick water body in a specially designed tub. Except legs, arms and the head, rest of the body is soaked in the water tub. It can also be done by lying over a wet towel folded lengthwise.

10. MUSCULAR RELAXATION

In the state of stress arising out of fear or anger, different muscles of the body get tensed; this makes a person more prone to anxiety. Through rhythmic contraction and relaxation, the tensed muscles can be stretched to their limits with associated release of tension and the muscles be brought to a relaxed and balanced state.

For muscular relaxation, carrying out certain practices of tensing and relaxing of muscles are very common. They can be performed in any comfortable position of sitting, standing or even lying over a mattress on the floor, preferably in an atmosphere which is quiet, safe and free from any distractions. While tensing the muscles of a particular area, breath has to be taken in and while releasing the muscle tension, the breath has to be released. After each activity of tensing and releasing of muscles, there should be a pause of around five seconds. Breathing in and breathing out should be normal without any pressure and should not take more that few counts.

Face – The eyebrows are to be pushed together, as though frowning followed by the muscles being relaxed. Next, the eyebrows are to be raised (as if startled) hard and then relaxed. This should be followed by clenching and releasing of the jaw muscles.

Neck – All the nerves connected to different organs and limbs of the body pass through the neck. The muscles of the neck and shoulder therefore accumulate lot of tension. The head is to be pressed back as hard as is comfortable and rolled slowly from side to side and then relaxed. This should be followed by gentle tilting of the head forward, pushing the chin towards the chest and then slowly lifting the head again.

Hands - The fist is to be clenched tightly for a few seconds followed by release of the tension. The exercise should be done for both the hands one after the other.

Arms - To tense the muscles of the arm, an elbow is to be bent for few seconds, followed by release of tensions in the muscles. This exercise should be done for both the hands, one after the other.

Chest - The whole of the lungs is to be filled through slow and deep abdominal breathing followed by slow release and evacuation of air from the lungs and then returning to normal breathing.

Stomach - The stomach muscles are to be tensed as tightly as possible followed by release of the tensed muscles.

Buttocks - The buttocks are to be squeezed together as much as possible followed by release of tension in the buttocks muscles.

Legs - The feet and toes is to be bent towards the face as hard as possible followed by releasing pressure on them to allow them to return back to their normal position. This should be followed by bending of the feet and toes away from the face for a few seconds followed by releasing pressure on them to allow them to revert back to their normal position.

Some of the Aasanas which help in releasing muscular tensions are greeva sanchalana, savasana, padmasana, sukhasana, shashankasana, naukasana and so forth. For general awareness of people, how these asanas are to be performed are discussed in the next section. It is however suggested that these asanas are learnt under the guidance of a teacher of proven credential and practiced for time durations as specified by him. There are variations in all these asanas which are to be carried out as advised by the teacher.

11. STRESS RELIEVING ASANAS

Greeva Sanchalana: 'Greeva' means neck and 'sanchalana' means movement. Neck movements are one of the most basic exercises in the yoga. It

- strengthens the muscles of the neck and the shoulders.
- releases tension, heaviness and stiffness in the head, neck and shoulder region.
- stimulates and provides relief to nerves of different organs (especially all sensory organs) that pass through the neck.

When all the movements involved in greeva sanchalan is performed slowly and rhythmically with slow and deep breathing, it calms and relaxes the mind. Primarily human neck makes the following six movements. All other movements are the products of the combination of these movements:

- Flexion
- Extension
- Right lateral rotation
- Left lateral rotation
- Right lateral flexion
- Left lateral flexion

Sitting relaxed in the cross legged position with the hands resting on the knees, spine remaining straight and eyes closed, the 'Greeva Sanchalana' can be performed in following different ways:

- Slowly moving the head forward as if trying to touch the chest with the chin. Then moving the head as far back as possible and comfortable without straining and trying to feel the stretch of the muscles of the neck all the way. Inhalation should be done during backward movement and exhalation during forward movement.
- With shoulder relaxed, slowly the head is to be moved to the right as if trying to touch the right ear to the right shoulder without raising the shoulders. Next, the head is to be moved to the left as if trying to touch the left shoulder with the left ear without straining in any way. More than the touching of ears to the shoulders focus on the movements to feel the stretch in the neck muscles is important. Here the upward movement is to be done during inhalation and the exhalation is to be done during downward movement.
- Gently the head is to be turned to the right as far as possible in a way that the chin is in line with the shoulder. The head then is to be moved to the left as far as possible without straining but feeling the movement of the neck all the way. In this variation, the inhalation is to be done while turning the head to the left or right and exhalation is to be done while returning to the zero position.
- Slowly the head is to be rotated downward, to the right, then upward and backward towards the left in a relaxed circular movement without feeling any strain but feeling the circular movement all the way. Inhalation is to be done when the head moves up and exhalation is to be done when the head moves down.

It can be performed at any time during the day, evening or even at night, on the bed, on the office chair, in the park or anywhere else.

Savasana: It

- releases stress, fatigue, depression and tension and improves concentration.
- cures insomnia and provides relaxation of muscles and the whole body.
- calms the mind, improves mental health and stimulates blood circulation."

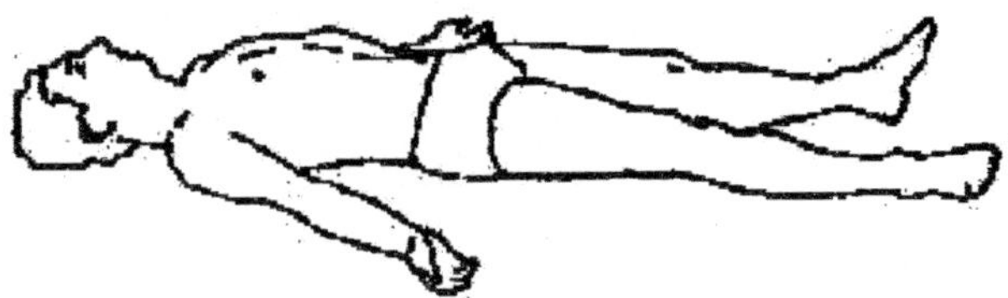

Figure no. 7 Savasana

Savasana is very helpful when a person feels physically and mentally exhausted. The practice of Savasana involves the following steps:

- Lying down flat on the back with arms about 15 cm away from the body with the palms facing upwards.
- To avoid discomfort, a thin pillow or a folded cloth may be placed behind the head. The fingers can be curled up slightly.
- The feet are to be kept slightly apart in a comfortable position with eyes closed.
- The head and spine are to be kept in a straight line.
- Care has to be taken to ensure that the head does not shift or fall on either side.

- The body is to be kept fully relaxed with no movements.
- The normal and natural breathing rhythm is to be maintained. After sometime revert back to the awareness of the body/surroundings and gently and smoothly get released from the posture.

During the practice of the above asana, there should not be even any slight movement in the body. It is effective after hard day's work. Higher the duration of practice the better will be the result. Ideally, it is to be practiced before sleep, before, during and after the breathing practices.

Padmasana: It is a cross-legged yoga asana. Major benefits arising out of this asana are:

- reduction in muscular tension.
- control on blood pressure.
- improvement in digestion.
- calming of the mind
- enabling for deep meditation and so forth.

Figure no. 8 Padmasana

Since the practice of Padmasana helps in overall blossoming of a person just like a lotus (padma flower), it is named as Padmasana. This asana is practiced in the following steps:

- Sitting with legs stretched out in front and keeping the spine in erect position.
- Bending the right knee and placing it on the left thigh making sure that the sole of the feet point upward and the heel is close to the abdomen.
- Bending the left knee and placing it on the right thigh making sure that the sole of the feet point upward and the heel is close to the abdomen.
- With both the legs crossed and feet placed on opposite thighs, both the hands are to be placed on the knees in mudra position.
- Mudra stimulates the flow of energy in the body. Padmasana has amazing effects when practiced with either chin mudra, chinmayi mudra, adi mudra or brahma mudra.
- Keeping the head straight and spine erect.
- Continuing with slow and deep breathing in and out.

This asana should not be practiced by a person till advised by a qualified teacher after flexibility of the knees are developed as per his instruction.

Sukhasana : It

- helps the nerves to calm down.
- provides the feelings of tranquility.
- improves concentration as the brain and all the sense organs in the head get a good supply of blood.

Figure no. 9 Sukhasana

Performance of Sukhasana embraces the following steps:

- Sitting on a mat with legs stretched out.
- Folding the left leg and tugging it inside the right thigh.
- Folding the right leg and tugging in inside the left thigh.
- Keeping the hands on the knees. Incorporation of jnana mudra or chin mudra in sukhasana is very effective during meditation.
- Sitting erect with spine straight.
- Relaxing the whole body and breathe slow and steadily.
- Remaining in the same position for as long as it is comfortable.

Sukhasana is the easiest and most comfortable of the meditation postures. It can be used for meditation even by those who are unable to sit comfortably in other asanas for meditation.

Shashankasana: It

- facilitates mental and physical balance without causing strain or pain.
- improves the circulation of blood to the scalp, face, and brain.
- helps in regulating the adrenal glands.

Figure no. 10 Shashankasana

Performance of Shashankasana involves the following steps:

- Sitting on Vajrasana i.e. kneeling down and placing the buttocks on the heels, knees together, toes overlapping and back straight with both palms placed on the knees.
- Keeping neck and spinal cord straight.
- Closing the eyes and concentrating on the breath.
- Taking deep breath and lifting the hands above the shoulders without bending the elbows. It is necessary at this stage to ensure maintenance of equal distance between the arms with the fingers raised.
- Slowly exhaling and bending down to touch the ground with the head and both the hands. This

step will be followed by simple relaxation when the forehead and palms touch the ground; during this period, some parts of the chest and abdomen will rest on the thighs.

- Allowing the upper torso to relax and remain in this position for a while making sure that the arms as well as the neck between the arms are kept straight.
- Exhaling slowly and reverting back to step one. This completes one cycle of Shashankasana.

Shashankasana is named so because the asana resembles the look of a hare in sitting position. This asana should not be practiced by those who have vertigo, slipped disc, high blood pressure or heart-related problems.

Naukasana: It

- stimulates the muscular, digestive, circulatory, nervous and hormonal systems.
- tones all organs and removes lethargy.
- is especially useful for eliminating nervous tension and restoration of deep relaxation.

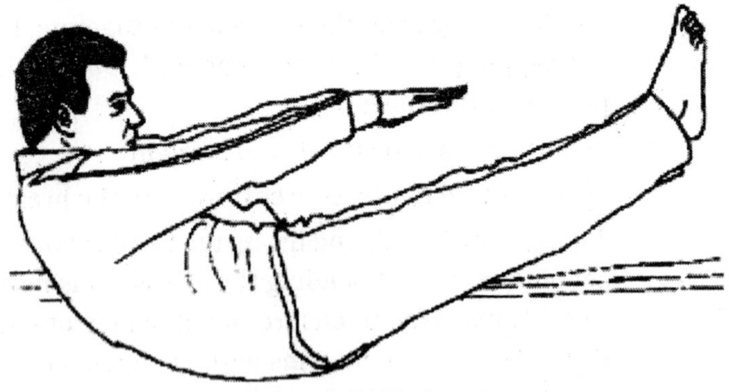

Figure no. 11 Naukasana

Performance of Naukasana involves the following steps:

- Lying on the floor on a mat with eyes open and looking upwards.
- Breathing in deeply and holding the breath while raising the legs, arms, shoulders, head and trunk off the ground.
- The shoulders and feet are not to more than 15 cms from the ground.
- Keeping the spine straight, the body is to be balanced on the buttocks.
- The arms are to be held at the same level and in line with the toes. The hands are to be kept open with the palms down and the look is to be focused towards the toes.
- Remain in this position by holding the breath and count at least five or more.
- Carefully returning to the starting position without injuring the head and relaxing after breathing out. This completes one round. At least 3 to five rounds are to be practised. Each round is to be followed by Savasana.

It should always be practiced under the guidance of a certified yoga teacher.

12. RELAXATION THROUGH BREATHING

Relaxation can be provided to the mind body complex through the adaptation of the following breathing practices:

- Simple abdominal breathing
- Pranayama

Simple abdominal breathing: Out of different types of breathing practices like-chest breathing, abdominal breathing, clavicular breathing etc. Abdominal breathing is considered to be the most important available tool among all for stress management. Controlled abdominal breathing has the potential to cause physiological changes that include:

- reduced blood pressure and heart rate
- reduced level of stress hormones in the blood
- reduced muscle tension
- improved activities of immune system
- increased feelings of calmness, well-being and so forth

Abdominal movements are prominent in abdominal breathing with little or no movement of the chest. For clear understanding of the process, figure no. 12 may be referred. The diaphragm in the figure is a dome shaped structure of muscles and fibrous tissues below the lungs; though not a part of the respiratory tract, it plays active role in the act of breathing. It separates the thoracic (chest) and abdominal cavities. During inhalation, when the diaphragm contracts the dome flattens and moves downward into the abdominal cavity. This movement increases the thoracic cavity; the increase being directly proportional to the extent of the 'movement' of reference. The diaphragm contraction also induces the lower ribs to move upward and forward, which further increases the thoracic volume.

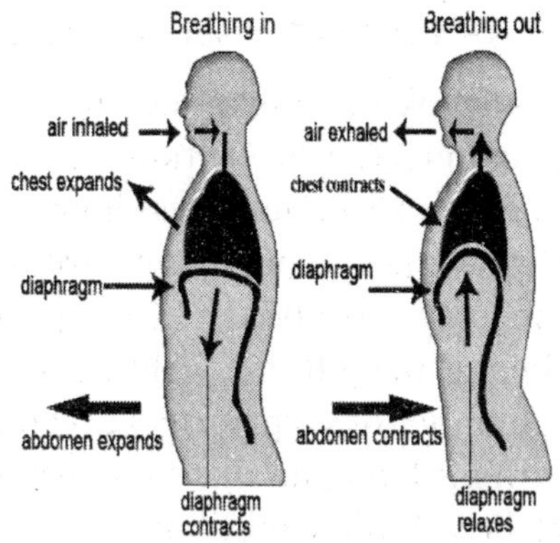

Figure no. 12

During exhalation, the diaphragm relaxes upwards, takes dome shape and allows the ribs to drop down and in with flattened belly and causes chest cavity to contract back to normal state.

To adapt abdominal breathing, a person must be aware of

- how he normally breathes.
- how abdominal breathing is done.

With the above knowledge, adapting to abdominal breathing becomes simpler; it only needs conscious and continuous practice. To know the pattern of his own breathing, a person has to relax and lie down flat on his back with the left hand on the chest and right hand on the navel area and follow each step of normal inhalation with full attention on the breath flowing

- in and out of the nose and mouth.
- in and out at the back of the mouth down to the throat.
- in and out of the throat area down to the trachea.

- in and out of the trachea through the bronchioles into the alveoli in the lungs.

While exhaling, the person again has to follow the breath flowing in the reverse direction from the alveoli in the lungs back to the atmosphere through the mouth and nasal openings.

Without exerting any extra effort, the above process of inhalation and exhalation has to be continued for few numbers of breathing cycles. With each cycle of breathing, the expansion and relaxation of the chest and downward and upward movement of the abdomen will be felt by the person through the rising and falling of the left and right hand respectively. After completing a number of such normal breathing cycles, if the person feels with his left hand that his chest expands and contracts with each breath while the abdominal area does not, then he is said to be on chest breathing or thoracic breathing. If on the other hand, the person feels with his right hand that his abdomen moves up and down with each breath with little or no movement of the chest, then the person is said to be on abdomen breathing or diaphragmatic breathing.

To consciously switch over to abdominal breathing, a person has to carry out the following in a sequential order:

- Lie down on the back with legs slightly bent from the knees.
- Place the right hand on the abdomen and left hand on the chest.
- Ensuring that there is no chest or shoulder movement, he subsequently has to start inhaling and exhaling feeling as if he is drawing the breath in and out through the navel.
- Inhalation should be through the nose and exhalation should be extended through mouth with pursed lip. In pursed lip technique the lip

usually is kept in a state resembling as if the person is whistling or attempting to flicker the flame of a candle.

- While inhaling the abdomen is to be expanded as much as possible, without expanding the rib cage. At the end of inhalation the diaphragm will be compressing the abdomen and the navel should be at its highest point.
- On exhalation, the diaphragm moves upwards and the abdomen moves downwards. At the end of exhalation, the abdomen will be contracted and the navel compressed towards the spine.
- To start with, the inhalation should be slow without exerting extra pressure with exhalation time being double of that of inhalation time. With more of practices, the duration of inhalation and exhalation can be increased.

Yoga practitioners gain control over their emotions by working with their breath. By learning to breathe gently, smoothly and without irregularities, they are able to address stressful and disturbed states of mind and bring them to calmness. Most of the practices of breathing that provide relaxation response to the body and the mind, fall under the techniques of Pranayamas in yogic parlance.

Pranayama: Simple abdominal breathing helps in learning of pranayama fast. Pranayama is slightly different from normal breathing. As per ancient Indian philosopher Patanjali, Pranayama is defined as *the regulation of the incoming and outgoing flow of breath with the additional dimension of retention.* So, unlike a normal breathing cycle which consists of two components, a cycle of Pranayama consists of three components, namely–

- Puraka i.e inhalation
- Rechaka i.e exhalation
- Kumbhaka i.e retention of breath

Puraka and Rechaka represent inhalation and exhalation, respectively of a normal breath. While Puraka involves application of energy with associated tensed muscles, Rechaka releases the tension in the muscles. Kumbhaka is the act of breath retention i.e. holding of breath. The act of Kumbhaka can be performed after–

- inhalation i.e. Puraka
- exhalation i.e. Rechaka
- each inhalation (Puraka) as well as each exhalation (Rechaka)

When retention of breath is done after inhalation, it is known as *inhalation retention* (also known as *antar Kumbhaka).*

When retention of breath is done after exhalation, it is known as *exhalation retention* (also known as *bahir or bahya Kumbhaka).*

If Kumbhaka is done after each Rechaka and each Puraka, the process is known as *Sahita Pranayama*.

Movements and distribution of prana in the human body under normal circumstances is unequal. This is essentially because from time to time prana moves and directs itself towards whichever part of the body has more demand for its specific fulfillment. Kumbhaka obviates the preferential movement of the prana and ensures its even distribution within the entire system of the body. During Kumbhaka all the senses get silenced and the concentration of the mind is enhanced which is so vital for achieving the ultimate state of meditation.

Proper practice of inhalation and exhalation to strengthen the lungs and balance the nervous and pranic systems through abdominal breathing is pre-requisite for a person before he initiates the act of learning Kumbhaka. It is suggested that to start with, the practice of Kumbhaka be done for a very short period and under the proper guidance of an experienced teacher. Subsequently, in gradual steps the 'duration' can be increased. The increase in the period of Kumbhaka should also be done under the active guidance of the teacher of reference above.

Those who achieve control over sahita pranayama can remain in Kumbhaka for a long stretch of time; they can even do away with Puraka as well as Rechaka and live only on the prana inside. In such a state, the practice is known as Kevala Pranayama. In Kavala pranayama, a person saves prana since it does not go out; if he remains in that state for say 10 minutes he saves 15 x 10 = 150 breaths (15 being the normal number of breaths per minute of a person) which is equivalent to 150 x 4 seconds = 600 seconds of his life (every normal breath takes 4 seconds of time on an average).

The very success of Pranayama depends on the maintenance of proper balance between Puraka, Rechaka and Kumbhaka. Pranayama is a proven breathing practice which guides a person to control and bring his wavering mind back to the state of homeostasis. There are different types of Pranayamas which play important role in providing relief to a person against stress arising out of fear or anger. Practices of specific Pranayamas in identified postures produce different energetic, mental, emotional and physical effects. A person needs to practice all these breathing techniques not only when he is under the grip of emotional attacks; he needs to practice them on a routine basis. Stress relieving Pranayamas include:

- Sheetali pranayama
- Nadi shodhana pranayma

- Ujjayi pranayama
- Bhramari pranayama
- Kapalbhati pranayama
- Bhrastika pranayama

For ease of understanding the above have been discussed in section 13 of chapter two. It however is suggested that these Pranayamas be learned under the guidance of a teacher of proven credential and practised for time durations as specified by him. There are variations in all these Pranayamas which are to be carried out as advised by the teacher.

13. STRESS RELIEVING PRANAYAMAS

Sheetali Pranayama: It

- has an overall cooling effect on the entire nervous system of the body.
- induces muscular relaxation, reduces mental and emotional excitation.
- is very effective in bringing an aroused body into a state of homeostasis.

The following steps are involved in Sheetali Pranayama:

- Sitting in a comfortable and upright position with spine straight, eyes closed, palms on knees and body relaxed.
- Extending the tongue outside the mouth. The tongue is then rolled from the sides so that it forms a narrow tube. The edges of the tongue should almost meet each other at the center on the top.
- Inhaling and filling the lungs slowly with abdominal breathing by drawing air through the tube formed by the tongue in the mouth.
- Pulling the tongue inside and closing the mouth.
- Bending the neck forward to do the chin lock (this is known as jalandhara bandha).
- Holding the breath (i.e. Kumbhaka) for some time without straining.
- Releasing jalandhara bandha and exhaling slowly through the nose.

The above completes one round of Sheetali Pranayama. The period of retention of breath i.e. Kumbhaka has to be increased in steps. Similarly the duration of inhalation, retention and exhalation also has to be gradually increased and adjusted. Number of rounds of practice needs to be increased gradually to at least 15 rounds under the guidance of a teacher.

Nadhi Shodhana Pranayama: It helps in relaxation by

- nourishing the whole body with extra supply of oxygen, efficient expulsion of carbon dioxide and removal of toxins from the body.
- bringing the wavering mind back to the present moment with increased vitality and lowered levels of accumulated stress and anxiety.
- harmonizing the left and right hemispheres of the brain, which correlate to the logical and emotional sides of human personality respectively.

Executions of Nadi Shodhana Pranayama embrace the following steps:

- Sitting comfortably with spine in erect position and shoulder relaxed.
- The left hand placed on the left knee with the tip of the thumb gently touching the tip of the index finger.
- The tips of the index and middle fingers of the right hand are to be placed in between the eyebrows.
- The ring and little finger of the right hand are to be placed on the left nostril (these two fingers will be used to open or close the left nostril).
- The thumb of the right hand is to be placed on the right nostril (this will be used for opening and closing of the right nostril).

- Sitting in the above posture, the first step of a cycle of Nadi Shodhana Pranayama involves closing of the right nostril with the thumb and breathing out through the left nostril. This is to be followed by breathing in through the left nostril with right nostril still closed by the thumb. Once it is done, the next step will be to hold the breath for few counts and then remove the thumb from the right nostril and breathe out through the right nostril after left nostril is closed by the ring and little finger.
- The second and the final step involve breathing in through the right nostril with left nostril still closed by the index and little finger. This will be followed by holding of breath and then exhalation through the left nostril after removing the index and little finger and closing of the right nostril by thumb.

The above cycle of alternate nostrils breathing is to be continued at least for nine rounds in a single sitting with long, deep, smooth and effortless breath without application of any forces (with eyes closed). The 'Kumbhaka' as well as different variations of Nadi Shodhona Pranayama should be practiced only under the guidance of a teacher of proven credential after being comfortable with the above practice without breath retention. This practice is never to be rushed or forced and breath is never to be taken through the mouth. Best time of practice is early morning before sunrise. It can however be done at any time except when the stomach is full.

Ujjayi Pranayama: It

- has a balancing influence on the entire cardio respiratory system and eases feelings of irritation and frustration with slowing down of heart rate,
- soothes the nervous system and calms the mind. It is also known as tranquilizing pranayama,
- has profound relaxing effect at the psychic level.

To create the ujjayi breathing, a person must constrict the back of the throat while inhaling and exhaling through the nostrils with lips remaining gently closed. The process is associated with audible sound often compared to the sound of the ocean. That is why ujjayi breathing sometimes is also referred to as '*ocean breath*'. The name ujjayi is derived from the Sanskrit word 'ujjayi,' which means '*to conquer*' or '*to be victorious*'. Ujjayi breathing is also known as '*victorious breath*' or '*hissing breath*'. Ujjayi stretches the breath, warms the inhaled air before it enters the lungs and this warmth unlocks the powerful healing process. To perform Ujjayi Pranayama, the following steps are involved:

- Sitting in a comfortable position with eyes closed.
- Concentrating on the nostrils, and allowing the breath to become calm and rhythmic.
- Concentration then has to be shifted to the throat with the imagination that breath is being drawn through throat not through nostrils.
- As the breathing becomes slower and deeper, the glottis has to be gently contracted so that a soft snoring sound like 'HHHHAAAA' is produced in the throat.
- Both inhalation and exhalation has to be long, deep and controlled and all along the sound from the throat is to be audible to the practitioner.
- The practice can start with ten breaths and then increased to five minutes. It can subsequently be enhanced to ten or twenty minutes.
- Only after the above is mastered, antar Kumbhaka is to be tried as per the guidance of a teacher of proven credential who can also provide help during adaptation of different 'variations'.

Ujjayi breathing can be performed in standing or in lying positions. Those suffering from slip disc or vertebral spondylitis may seek expert practitioner's advice and perform it in Vajrasana or Makarasana.

Bhramari Pranayama: It enables a person to

- get relieved of his stress and cerebral tension when the mind is buzzing with cross thoughts.
- alleviate anger and anxiety.
- induce a meditative state by harmonizing the mind and directing his awareness inward.

The humming sound produced during the practice has soothing effect on the mind and the nervous system.

Execution of Bhramari Pranayama involves the following steps:

- Sitting comfortably in a quiet and well ventilated place with eyes closed and hand resting on the knees with body fully relaxed.
- The lips are kept gently closed with teeth slightly separated so that the sound vibrations are heard and felt distinctly throughout the practice.
- With arms raised sideways and elbows bent, the hands are to be brought to the ears.
- Index fingers or the middle fingers are to be used either to plug the ears by inserting the fingers on the ear hole or to press the ear flaps without inserting the fingers in the ear hole.
- During inhalation and exhalation, the concentration always has to be on the ajna chakra (the place between the eye brows). Inhalation should be done through the nose.
- After a deep inhalation, exhalation is to be done slowly in a controlled manner making all the way

a deep, steady humming sound like that of a black bee. The humming should be even and continuous during the entire period of exhalation. The sound should be soft and mellow to make the front of the skull to reverberate.

- At the end of the exhalation, the hands are to be returned to the knees and then raised again for the next breath. The above completes one round of breathing.

Five to ten rounds of breathing is good enough to start with. With time and practice this can be increased further. In case of extreme mental tension or anxiety, the practice can be increased to even thirty minutes. To relieve mental tension, Bhramari Pranayama can be practised at any time of the day; best time of practice however is early morning or late at night when the environment is noiseless. Once the above is mastered, Kumbhaka and different variations can be learned under the guidance of a teacher of proven credential.

Kapalbhati Pranayama: It helps a person to

- soar his energy level when he feels low on it. It also aids in resolving respiratory disorder and calming down of the mind in preparation for meditation. In fact its energizing effect is such that one does not easily fall asleep while sitting on meditation.
- purify the nadis (the conduits of the flow of subtle prana, the vital energy in the human body) and tone his digestive systems,
- remove sensory distractions, balance and strengthen his nervous system

Execution of Kapalbhati Pranayama involves the following steps:

- Sitting in a comfortable position, with head and spine in straight position with hands resting on the knees.
- Focussing on the flow of breath with eyes closed and body relaxed without application of external force.
- Exhalation has to be done through both nostrils with a forceful contraction of the abdominal muscles. The following inhalation has to be taken passively by allowing the abdominal muscles to relax.
- The inhalation has to be a spontaneous recoil, without involving additional effort.
- After completion of ten rapid breaths in succession, the inhalation and exhalation has to be made deeper. The breath then has to be allowed to return to normalcy.
- The above completes one round of breathing. To start with at least five rounds of breaths must be practiced.
- The rapid breathing has to be from the abdomen, with shoulder and face remaining in relaxed position. The beginners however can take free normal breaths between the rounds and increase their breathing from ten counts to fifty counts once the abdominal muscles become stronger.

Once the above process is mastered, the practice of Kumbhaka should be incorporated and different 'variations' be tried as per the guidelines of a teacher of proven credential. The practice of Kapalbhati Pranayam also known as '*frontal brain cleansing breath*' should be performed on an empty stomach or at least three to four hours after meals. Kapalbhati Pranayama should not be practiced by those suffering from heart disease, high blood pressure, vertigo, hernia or gastric ulcer.

Bhrastika Pranayama: It

- increases vitality and lowers the stress and anxiety levels.
- it helps in clearing blockages (if any) in the passageway of pranaic flow through the subtle nadis and in opening of sushumna nadi for prana to flow through it.
- balances and strengthens the nervous system, induces peace, tranquility and one-pointedness of mind in preparation for meditation.

To perform Bhastrika Pranayama, the following steps are involved:

- Sitting in a comfortable posture with hands placed on the knees.
- Staying relaxed with focus on the breathing pattern with head and spine straight.
- Taking a deep breath in and breathing out forcefully through the nose. Inhalation has to be forceful through both the nostrils making sure that the lungs are full with air. The exhalation also has to be done with application of force making a hissing sound. Forceful inhalation results from full expansion of the abdominal muscles and forceful exhalation from contraction of the abdominal muscles without straining.
- How much force is to be applied during inhalation and exhalation is to be determined by the individual's health and endurance power.
- Applied force is needed to be increased gradually by maintaining equal force of inhalation and exhalation.

- During inhalation, the diaphragm descends and the abdomen moves outward. During exhalation the diaphragm moves upward and the abdomen moves inward.
- The practice is to be repeated for ten breaths to complete one round. Gradually the breathing has to be increased to five rounds.

The practice of Bhastrika Pranayama is to be performed every day. With acclimatization, breathing speed can be enhanced without compromising on rhythm. It is also known as '*bellow breath*' as air is drawn forcefully in and out of the lungs like the bellows of a village blacksmith. Practice of Kumbhaka and its different variations should always be performed under the guidance of a proven practitioner in gradual steps. Those who have high blood pressure or heart disease should not practice Bhastrika Pranayama.

14. RELAXATION THROUGH MEDITATION

Human mind keeps wandering here and there with cross thoughts mostly embracing either the past or the future with very little tendency to remain focused in the present moment. Meditation is a discipline that turns the mind and attention inward; it basically aims at bringing the wavering mind into the present and in a state of calmness. This reduces the stress producing activity of the mind to a great extent. It is relevant to quote *Lord Buddha* in this context. Once on being asked what he gained through meditation, he said, *"Nothing! However, let me tell you what I have lost – anger, anxiety, depression, insecurity, fear of old age and death".*

Two types of meditation techniques are very common:

(i) Focussed attention meditation

(ii) Open monitoring meditation

Focused attention meditation: In this process, the attention is focused on a single object during the entire session of meditation. The object may be:

- the breath
- visualization of a part of body or external object
- mental repetition of mantra

Through regular practice, a person is able to improve his depth and steadiness of focused attention meditation. The practice of pranayama falls in the category of focused attention meditation in which the focus remains on the breath. During the practice of pranayama, when the word A-U-M is chanted at each of the chakras during Rechaka as well as Puraka, the process of Pranayama gets deeper and deeper and eventually leads a person towards experiencing that all his senses are stilled.

Open monitoring meditation: In open monitoring meditation, instead of focusing the attention on anything specific, a person keeps the mind open and monitors all aspects of his experiences without any judgment or attachment. The practicing person in this process becomes an observer to all his perceptions and recognizes and sees them for what they are irrespective of whether the perceptions are internal (like thought, feeling, memory etc.) or external (like sound, smell etc.). The meditating person in this process observes with non attachment the working of his own mind and begins to have an increasing awareness about how his change of thoughts bring about changes in his emotions. In other words he observes which thought makes him happy and which thought makes him unhappy.

'Vipassana' falls in the category of open monitoring meditation. It is basically a way of self-transformation through self-observation. Vipassana meditation rediscovered by Gautam Buddha some 2500 years ago essentially is a process to see things as they really are. It is this observation-based, self-exploratory journey to the common root of the mind-body complex that dissolves mental impurity and results in a balanced mind full of love and compassion. Performing 'Vipasana' meditation involves various steps. It should always be learned and practiced under the guidance of a teacher.

While meditating, a time comes when the attention of the person is not focused on anything in particular but is reposed on quietude; in this state, a person becomes thoughtless. This state is known as a state of '*no mind*'. The processes of '*focussed attention meditation*' and '*open monitoring meditation*' in reality are the means to train the mind, which ultimately leads a person towards achieving this deeper state of consciousness. When such a state is achieved, a person's five senses get stilled, his intellect gets stilled and he enters a state of oneness where there is no happiness and no unhappiness. In this state a person fails to express himself but enjoys a unified experience and that experience does not change with circumstances or environment. This is the ultimate of true meditation which leads towards spiritual consciousness. The practice of all types of meditation should always be learned and practiced under the guidance of a teacher of proven credential.

Chapter Three

FEAR & ITS DIFFERENT FACES

Fear is an emotion induced by a threat perception. Fundamentally it is a perceptual evaluation of a stimulus which may be real but more often it is psychological. It makes a person sense that some loss or harm is going to be caused to him by a stimulus which can either be internal or external. Like the stars in the sky, fear triggering stimuli is countless. Even self talks trigger threat perception. When a person constantly thinks of fear, he literally invites fear to make its home in his mind. Fear does not follow similar patterns of response from every human being. Under the influence of identical stimuli, different people perceive different intensities of fear. Even the same person at different moments can have different intensities of fear perceptions under the influence of the same stimulus. Fear can be mild, medium, or intense. The feelings of fear can be brief as well as long lasting. Fear has the potential to generate stress which in turn causes Fight or Flight response that enables a person to get prepared either to fight the stressor or flee away from it. If this response however persists for long or occurs frequently, it can do lot of damages to a person physically as well as mentally.

To keep fear under control and deal with it effectively, it is always desired that the mind is kept rational, active and in a state of balance through adaptation of various relaxation techniques. Fears are mostly learned, so they can be unlearned and a new learning be acquired instead. This however requires lots of understanding and introspections with awareness of various aspects of fear and different ways to deal with them. The biggest tool through which a person most effectively can deal with fear is 'belief' – both on self as well as on Almighty. Those who believe that fears are surmountable and explore all means to find a way to combat them, eventually succeed in achieving their goal.

15. ROLE OF FEAR IN HUMAN LIFE

Fear is not necessarily cause based; it is also perceived even when the expected events or circumstances do not exist or have chances of occurring in reality. The following story is relevant in this context.

"There was a woman who had a tendency to get worried over even small issues. She was once asked by one of her friends to keep custody of a casket for few days when the friend planned an outstation trip. The casket contained a diamond bracelet. Out of fear, to ensure additional safety, the woman immediately went to a jeweller's shop to purchase a stronger casket to keep the bracelet. She briefed the jeweller about her need and also showed him the bracelet as well as the casket. Checking the bracelet the jeweller told the lady, 'The diamonds of the bracelet are artificial. You need not worry so much about purchasing another casket for its additional safety.' Hearing this, the lady heaped a sigh of relief and said, 'Thank God, my worries are over'."

The above is the reality of life. The above corroborates the old adage that many of the human miseries lie in anticipation only. The reason for the above can be attributed to the fact that majority of the people lack in sufficient knowledge about what scares them and also why they are scared of what they do not know.

When human brain is given only a few pieces of information, it tends to fill in the rest of the details by itself often with messages of worst consequences. This is how most of the fears that never materialize are given births. Imagination always magnifies the fear perception manifold.

Fear has the potential to play positive as well as negative role in human life; it all depends on how a person deals with it. On the positive side, feeling afraid is helpful in certain situation. It signals danger and alerts people to prepare themselves to effectively deal with the anticipated 'fear'. If a person does not get scared under certain circumstances, he would end up doing things that would increase his risk of suffering in future and in some cases may even endanger his life. As an alarm, fear always provides an opportunity to a person to make preparations against anticipated threats in advance. It is relevant to quote *Napoleon Bonaparte* in this context. He was once asked if he feared bad luck. He replied in affirmative and said, *"I believe that I shall have it, and I prepare myself accordingly."* Napoleon's reply had lot of messages within. What he really meant through his reply was that in anticipations, he always identified possible threats and prepared himself against those. This is the reason why he was always said to have been found to be ready for any occasion.

Unlike Napoleon, most of the people in general are not able to anticipate and figure out possible threats or remain passive or complacent even after they get fear signals. Some even buckle down under the pressure of the perceived threat. This happens either because of lack of total knowledge that many people have about 'fear' or because of their 'ignorance' about how to deal with them. Unless a person knows what scares him and why, he will never be able to deal with it appropriately. Ignorance often leads to complacency. Complacency is the feelings of contentment without the awareness of self deficiency and knowledge of upcoming problem. Complacency dulls a person's senses and becomes an impediment to his preparedness against any upcoming event.

In the above context, it is interesting to quote boxing legend *George Foreman*. After losing to Mohammad Ali, he said, *"In boxing, I had a lot of fear. Fear was good. But, for the first time, in the bout with Muhammad Ali, I didn't have any fear. I thought, 'This is easy. This is what I've been waiting for'. No fear at all. No nervousness. And I lost."* Having fear is good when a person takes cue from it and prepares himself to face an upcoming event in his life.

Fear has the potential to contribute positively in the growth and development of a person in many ways; some of those are mentioned underneath:

- Fear of hurting someone can make a person more conscious.
- Fear of failure can make a person more keen and dynamic.
- Fear can move a person from carelessness to taking care.
- Fear can move a person from being insensitive to being sensitive.
- Fear can move a person from dullness to alertness.

Fear activates human stress mechanism which causes the body to respond physiologically in 'Fight or Flight' mode. On an immediate basis this response helps a person to prepare either to fight or flee away from the fear perception. When the 'Fight or Flight' response persists for a long stretch of time or occurs frequently, it has the potential to cause mental and physical harm to a person in the long term (refer section 09 of chapter two). Extreme cases of stress and tension arising out of fear can even cause immobility (full or partial) to a person. Fear has the negative potential to

- interfere with the ability of a person to think clearly, speak with steady voice and keep his mind steady.

- create indecisiveness that results in stagnation. Many talented people are often found to procrastinate indefinitely basically in order to avoid the risk of a possible failure. In the process they lose opportunities with attended erosion of confidence.
- rob a person of his joys, contentment and peace of mind. When a person is repeatedly under 'fear syndrome', his life becomes centered on pessimism and gloom.
- eat into a person's present . To numb the pain of overbearing distress and foreboding arising out of fear, people often turn to things like drugs and alcohol for artificial relief; in the process they often become 'addicted' in the long run.
- make a person feel anxious, nervous, worried or panic.
- even turning a person into its slave with devastating results.

Anxiety is the feelings of uneasiness about something which is perceived to have an uncertain future outcome. It is caused when a person tries to find certainty in uncertain situation. It usually is a response to outside forces. However, there are people who make themselves anxious with 'negative self talk' too – a habit of always telling 'self' that the worst is going to happen. Anxiety is often accompanied by muscular tension, restlessness, fatigue and problems in concentration. If experienced on regular basis, a person may suffer from an anxiety disorder.

Feelings of inadequacy are the starting point of **nervousness.** It is normally activated before an event or in circumstances where a person has to prove his worth, like appearance before an interview board, answering question in meetings, or delivering a speech before a large gathering and so forth.

Nervousness is generated out of a person's own feelings of self inadequacy and is an indicator of his lack of self confidence.

Unlike anxiety and nervousness which are short time phenomena, **worry** is a long time condition. It does not arise out of sudden and specific stimulus as in the case of anxiety and nervousness. Worry often embraces future. Since the future is yet to be born, it cannot easily be determined or ascertained. This leads to imagination of many 'what ifs'. In unknown circumstances, people generally have the tendency to settle on the most catastrophic outcome; often on the basis of past bad experiences. This is how the 'unknown' magnifies worries. Since the past is already gone and the future is yet to come, if a person worries too much, it will only ruin his present.

It is a general observation that people who worry excessively are so anxiety-ridden that they seek relief through harmful life style habits such as overeating, use of alcohol, drugs etc. These people develop the tendency to dwell on their perceived worries most of the time and become prone to experiencing uncomfortable physical symptoms like fatigue and sore muscles. A worried person often has problem with 'sleep' and 'concentration'.

Panic is caused by sudden surge of overwhelming anxiety and fear. It basically is an extension of fear in extreme form; it is triggered when a person is faced with a life threatening situation. It can occur at random or in situations where a person is exposed to certain events that trigger panic to him. The panic alert instantly gets the body in Fight or Flight response either to face the situation or flee from it.

16. BASIC CAUSES OF FEAR

Basic causes of fear can broadly be classified into the following categories:

I. Fear of extinction
II. Fear of mutilation
III. Fear of loss of autonomy
IV. Fear of separation
V. Fear of ego hurt

I. **Fear of extinction:** The following are some of the examples of fear of extinction:

- Fear of being shot or murdered
- Fear of nuclear war and mass destruction
- Fear of being caught and burnt alive in a fire
- Fear of being killed in a bomb blast
- Fear of air crash

Some people often simultaneously experience the fear of extinction and mutilation. For example, a person looking downwards from the edge of a high rise building generally undergoes the fear of extinction as well as the fear of mutilation.

Fear of extinction basically is the fear of ceasing to exist i.e. fear of death. The worry about dying, generally circles around the following self interrogations of most of the individuals:

- What will happen to my family after I am gone?
- How my death will affect the life of my children and grandchildren?

- How my spouse will be able to recover from the shock of my death?
- Whether I shall have a peaceful or a painful death?
- Where will I go after my death?

While people can't control when or how they leave this world, they certainly can control much of what they leave behind for their near and dear ones for their sustenance. They feel a sense of relief when they get their acts in order while living a healthy life. They know that, should the inevitable happen, their wishes will be fulfilled and their legacy secure. Whether a person will die in pain or will experience a peaceful death depends to a large extent on his karma while alive.

The fear of of being no longer arouses a primary existential anxiety in all normal humans. This is in spite of the fact that everyone is aware that any other thing presumed to be happening in this world may or may not eventually happen in reality, but that a person born on earth has to die is an absolute truth. To overcome the fear of death, it is absolutely necessary that a person knows the reality of death.

Death is the separation of human consciousness (atma or soul) from the physical body. Human physical body can be compared to a car and the soul or atma to its driver. For seeing the road, the car has head light, mankind sees through their eyes. The car makes sound through its horn, mankind talks. The car has four wheels; each man has two legs and two hands. The car moves from one place to another, mankind can also move from one place to another. The moment the driver gets down from a car, all the car activities mentioned above stop; the car cannot move even an inch. Same happens to the mankind when atma leaves the physical body. The moment the atma of a person leaves his body, he cannot see, talk or move; he becomes a dead body. The soul however does not die; after leaving one body, it takes shelter in another body just like a driver gets down from one car and gets on to another car and drives it.

Death can be compared to sleep. Sleep is but a short death which everybody enjoys and welcome. Sleep lasts only for few hours. Whereas death may last for longer time, and when a person wakes up, instead of having the same body, he finds himself in a new body. If death is little more than waking after an extended sleep, why should anyone worry over 'death'? Death gives people a new life, a new chance and fresh hopes. It allows people to go back home, to their real abode. In this context, it is relevant to quote the following *Bengali song written by Sri Ayodhyanath Pakrashi* which Swami Vivekananda sang during his early days when he met Sri Ramkrishna Paramahanshadev.

"Mon cholo nijo niketone,
Songshar bideshe bideshir beshe
Bhromo keno okarone
Mon cholo nijo niketone."

It means—

Let us go back once more, O mind, to our own abode!
Here in this foreign land of earth
Why should we wander aimlessly in stranger's guise?

Let us go back once more, O mind, to our own abode!

II. Fear of mutilation: It is the fear of losing a part of the body or even the natural functions of various organs of the body. Even the thought of having his body's boundaries invaded externally causes fear of mutilation in a person. The following are some of the examples of fear of mutilation:

- Fear of train or road accidents
- Fear of attack by animal
- Fear of physical assault by someone

- Fear of fall from a height
- Fear of leakage of poisonous gases, exposure to radioactivity etc.

III. **Fear of loss of autonomy:** It is the fear of a person of being immobilized, paralyzed, restricted, entrapped, imprisoned or otherwise dictated by circumstances beyond his control. In physical form, it's commonly known as claustrophobia. It is not necessarily a congested environment but often the feelings of what will happen to a person when he is confined in a specific area that triggers the fear of loss of autonomy. Common examples of fear of loss of autonomy are:

- fear of elevators
- fear of crowded areas
- fear of car break down in a remote place where no help is available
- fear of tunnels, subway trains etc

Fear of loss of autonomy also extends to human social interactions and relationships, like fear of intimacy. With intimacy, fear of loss of autonomy also grows. Every person before becoming close to another person forms an image of the other person in the mind. If that image matches to his imagination of a good person then he starts liking that person. With more and more time spent together, mutual attachment grows. Attachment again is associated with fear. When a person is closely attached to another person he is always apprehensive of

- losing the acceptance of the other person,
- the possible change in the thinking pattern of the other person,

- the possible change in the feelings and behavior of the other person towards him.

IV. **Fear of separation:** It is the fear of abandonment, rejection, loss of connectedness etc. Such fears can have a devastating psychological effect on a person; they generally arise when a person starts feelings that he is not wanted, respected, or valued by others. The following are some of the examples of fear of separation:

- Fear of separation from the children in old age
- Fear of criticism/comments from others in work area
- Fear of losing job
- Fear of being left alone in old age after the death of the partner
- Fear of rejection by others (this is also partly associated with fear of ego hurt).

A blunt retaliation against criticism does not lead a person towards any solution. Criticism needs to be analyzed and introspected with a broader perspective; especially because many times a person unwittingly fails to notice certain defects in himself which are brought to light through criticism. Criticisms often act as a mirror which enables the person to see dirt on his face (if any) which otherwise cannot be seen. To keep the tolerance level of anger under control against criticism, a wise man rightly said, *"Don't mind criticism. If it is untrue, disregard it; If it is unfair, keep away from irritations; If it is ignorant, smile.; If it is justified, learn from it."*

V. **Fear of ego hurt:** It is the fear of humiliation, shame etc. It basically arises out of the fear of shattering or disintegration of a person's sense of capability, worthiness etc. It includes:

- Fear of lagging behind competitors
- Fear of public speaking
- Fear of insult or being ridiculed by others
- Fear of getting punishment after a work
- Fear of failure in interviews, examinations etc

It is the fear of ego hurt which is responsible for the development of self perceived fears. When self perceived fears start dictating human actions, they have adverse affect on a person's life. People with self perceived fear develop the tendency to avoid exposures to events and circumstances. This is mainly because of their perception and apprehension that people are watching each of their actions as well as the results of the actions with a view to criticize them whenever they fail. Though this is not the reality, it often makes them avoid exposure, decision making as well as direct facing of the reality.

Those who let their thoughts, feelings and decisions to be influenced and driven by self perceived fear, often find that their life is more of a byproduct of fear, rather than that of their own desires; they fail to make full utilization of their potentials.

As long as a person let his self-perceived fears permeate or as long as he runs away instead of facing and confronting them with preparedness after deep introspection, they will continue to haunt him. Running away gives a person an illusion of security that too only for short periods. Every moment a person spends swirling around in self perceived fear, he cultivates a seed that gives rise to similar thoughts. The more he does, the more he is set back by it; in the process instead of calmly dealing with the situation and rationally identifying solutions to move ahead, he feeds and wastes energy into something not constructive.

Self-perceived fears are seldom life threatening. They are all made up in the mind. For example, detailed introspection of the fear of public speaking (a top ranked self-perceived fear amongst majority of people) reveals that it basically springs up from the possible thought of being embarrassed or humiliated by others. Before public speaking, the following thoughts generally come up in the mind of a person:

- "What happens if I'll forget the speech?"
- "What happens if the presentation will go wrong?"
- "What happens if the audiences will start feeling bored?" and so forth.

May be none of the above had happened in the past. And even if anything had happened in the past, it does not mean that it is going to happen in the future too. The reality is, even if the worst that a person contemplates do take place, the heaven will not fall on earth; he will continue to live like any other person in this world with options open for bringing about improvements from every corner. Since the above is the reality, why should every person not introspect and introspect not only to lessen the burden of 'self perceived fears' but also to evolve strategies and implement them to overcome them.

17. FEARS ARE MOSTLY LEARNED

Though it appears really confusing and embarrassing when a person is seen to be afraid of things that others seem to have no problem with, it cannot be termed as a sign of his weakness or immaturity. It is simply a learned response stored in his brain. People are born with fear of fall and fear of noise inbuilt in their DNA. Other than these two, all other types of fears are learned either through self-experience or from the experience of associates or others.

Learned knowledge in any sphere of life can always be replaced by a new learning. This however does not happen automatically; it involves the process of unlearning the first learning and then learning a new learning (this is known as *relearning*).

The above gives the confidence that when a person's learned knowledge about a fear becomes painful or unacceptable to him because of demands of circumstances, he can replace it by new knowledge acquired through appropriate technique. The above however, warrants that the person:

- has a thorough understanding and knowledge of his specific fear.
- knows exactly why he wants to come out from its grip.
- knows clearly what is the new knowledge he is going to acquire to replace his current fear perception.
- is clear about how the new learning is going to be helpful to him in the long run.

- is clear about how the new knowledge can be acquired.

The knowledge about what a person fears and also why, and the introspection of all the fearful incidences that he had experienced in the past reduces the level of his fear and also the degree of worries associated with it. It also helps him a lot in formulating strategies to effectively manage specific fear. Additional knowledge on if the occurrence of the specific fear is a recurring phenomenon that interferes with normal life or occurs once in a while and does not necessarily interfere with normal life, also provides help to a great extent during problem solving and action initiating stages against a perceived fear.

Learned/acquired fears can broadly be classified into three categories.

- Internal fear
- Sub-conscious fear
- External fear

Recognizing the category in which a person's fear fits into, is absolutely necessary for him to work out the action plans of how to deal with it. In general, external fear is relatively easier to overcome compared to internal fear and the subconscious fear.

Internal fears are triggered by external factors, but unlike external fears, they are not specific to any circumstance or event. For example, the fear of failure can crop up in the mind of a person in different situations such as when he

- starts a business
- participates in a competition
- appears in an interview for promotion and so forth.

Internal fears arise out of internal feelings, they remain mostly hidden and are therefore difficult to recognize. Internal fears create feelings of self-doubt, and are often the cause of a person's low self-esteem. A person with internal fear generally develops the feeling that he is incapable of doing and achieving anything, as a result, most of the time he does not even make a start to do something. Even if, the person eventually initiates action to start doing something, he does so half heartedly.

A person who had been disciplined, criticized or punished quite often during his childhood and formative years (when human mind is developing and most impressionable) by his parents, teachers etc. generally develop low self esteem in later years. Negative experiences in life also contribute towards development of low self esteem.

The funniest thing is majority of the people feel that they do not have any internal fear though circumstances in reality reveal that they have many. Unless people introspect and do exploration to bring to surface what causes them fear and why, they will continue to feel that they are free from internal fears while others have them and keep judging and in some cases even criticizing others.

Subconscious fear basically is a type of internal fear. A sub-conscious fear is rooted deep inside a person, and is generally caused by some sort of limiting belief about himself or the world around him. When a person consciously and repeatedly thinks that he has some shortcomings, those thinking get ingrained into his system and are stored in the subconscious mind. Subsequently they spark into action through external stimulation. When subconscious fears become beliefs, people often fail to identify them as fears. Living with subconscious fear is always harmful. It unwittingly brings limitations towards a person's utilization of self-potential and often causes anxiety for him. Some of the examples of subconscious fears are:

- Fear of losing acceptance of people;
- Feear of losing respect,
- Fear of being wrongly interpreted,
- Fear of losing trust of people;
- Fear of losing psychological security etc.

External fears are triggered by specific external circumstances or objects. External fear is easily recognized, and is caused to a person mostly due to some of the traumatic events in the past experienced by him or some of his close associates. Person, who got bit by a lizard at a young age, is likely to develop the tendency to consciously avoid facing lizard when he grows up.

Phobia is an external fear in which a person has an irrational fear of typical situations, living creatures, places or things, despite the awareness and reassurance that it is not dangerous. Even the phobic persons are also aware that their perception of fear is much greater in their mind than in real life; even then they tend to avoid phobic sources.

The main difference between fear and phobia lies in the intensity and severity of the emotions experienced. If confronted with the source of phobia, a phobic person undergoes intense stress which often turns into panic. The very thought of phobia also makes some phobic person immensely distressing. A phobic person consciously tries to avoid coming across such things for which he has phobia. For example, if a person has the phobia of dog, he may even feel afraid to walk in a specific road even if there is no dog on the way. When phobia interferes with the normal life activities of a person, it needs to be addressed through proper technique or techniques.

Phobia can be classified into two different types:

(I) Simple phobias

(II) Complex phobias

(I) **Simple phobias** are characterized by persistent disproportionate fears about specific objects, living creatures, activities, situations etc. Following are some of the examples of simple phobia:

- *Glossophobia:* It is the fear of speaking in front of an audience.
- *Claustrophobia:* It is the fear of enclosed or tight spaces.
- *Aviatophobia:* It is the fear of flying.
- *Dentophobia:* It is the fear of the dentist or dental procedures.
- *Hemophobia:* It is the fear of blood or injury
- *Animal or insect phobias:* The most common amongst animal/insect phobias are arachnophobia (fear of spiders), cynophobia (fear of dogs), and ophidiophobia (fear of snakes), nyctophobia (fear of the night time or darkness).

(II) **Complex phobias** are deep-rooted fears about particular circumstances. They can broadly be classified into:

- Social phobia
- Agoraphobia

Social phobias: People with social phobia find it difficult to become a part of social situations. They generally avoid public speaking, attending parities or interactions with others. Those with social phobia are always apprehensive of being embarrassed or humiliated in public. They are afraid of

- talking in public
- acting in stage in front of big crowd

- being laughed at because of their clothes, voice or some features of their body

Agarophobias: Persons suffering from agarophobia are frightened of finding themselves in congested places. The word '*agoraphiobia*' itself refers to '*fear of open spaces*'. It is basically a fear about places or situations from which one cannot escape. Generally agoraphobic persons are afraid of

- travelling in public bus or train
- visiting large shops or shopping malls etc.

Agoraphobics generally, are prone to being social phobic too. Agoraphobia may eventually lead to loneliness and depression.

Observations of phobic experiences of parents or seniors during childhood and traumatic experiences during formative years often turn into phobia in grown up years. Phobias can also be caused by genetic and environmental reasons.

18. SUPPRESSION & EXPRESSION OF FEAR

It is often seen that even when nothing is threatening or disturbing, there are occasions when people get feared by fear. Fear of fear probably causes more fear in human lives than the fear itself. *Ex. President of U.S.A, Franklin Roosevelt,* was spot on when he said, *"The only thing we have to fear is the fear itself."*

Once a fear crops up in the mind, it demands attention. On an instant basis belief on the saying *"this too shall pass"* or switching focus and concentration on something of interest, like listening to music etc. can provide relief to a fearful person, but such reliefs are only temporary in nature.

There are people, who on experiencing the feeling of fear decide not to dwell on them internally by continuously thinking about them or express them externally by acting it out. What they do in fact is, try to suppress the feelings of fear. Externally, they pretend to be absolutely normal but internally, to divert their attention from the thoughts of the feared objects/events, they sometimes even resort to numb their mental activities through drinking of alcohol, usage of drugs etc. or keep their mind occupied with excessive work, reading, listening to music and so forth.

The tendency to suppress the feelings of fear develops in people due to various reasons. Some of them are mentioned below:

- When people think that probably it is not normal for them to express their feeling in a certain way as others might construe this as their sign of weakness.

- When people think that their expressions of feelings of fear may not be viewed positively by their seniors or employers.
- When due to their traumatic past experiences, people are not sure about how to react.
- When people consciously try to avoid undergoing the feelings of rejection, hardship, failure, shame, guilt, loss of self esteem etc.
- When people think that no one understands them and they themselves will have to do everything to get out from there. Wittingly or unwittingly they take the route of 'suppression'.

Suppression is never a solution of fear. It might provide immediate relief to a person from the clutch of the intense feelings of fear but such reliefs are only temporary in nature. 'Suppression' eventually in the form of 'repression' simply pushes the 'feelings of fear' of a person to his sub-conscious mind where it sits and waits, until another bout of stimulus triggers it to resurface again with more intense feelings. It is relevant to quote *Sigmund Freud* in this context. He said, *"Unexpressed emotions will never die. They are buried alive and will come forth later in uglier ways."* In the above context, it is to be noted that repression basically is the same thing as suppression, except that once the disturbing and distressing thoughts are repressed unlike in the case of suppression, they are pushed into relatively inaccessible areas in the subconscious mind. In repression, people lose conscious awareness of the thoughts which gets practically swallowed by the subconscious mind till they explode with multiplied adverse effects.

Suppression of fear interrupts normal flow of energy in the body's energy system. With suppression of fear, a person is forced to swallow low energy of vibration in his body; in the short term this causes him to

- undergo depression without apparent cause
- walk around with a knot in stomach and tightness in throat
- blow up even over minor incidents
- lack in motivation
- experience troubled personnel relationships with family, friends, acquintances etc. and so forth

In the long run, suppressed fear has the potential to cause hardening of arteries, stiffening of joints, weakening of bones, undermining of the immune systems etc. It can even make a person vulnerable to different types of serious illnesses.

The best way to respond to fear is to face it outright (of course with a well thought out action plans). It is relevant to mention the following anecdote in this context.

'Swami Vivekananda was once walking along a footpath in Benaras. All of a sudden, he turned back and noticed that few monkeys were following him. He got scared and started moving faster. Seeing the monkeys still following him at faster pace, he started running. An old passerby, who was watching Swami Vivekananda and his plight from a distance, caught his hand and asked him to turn back, face and chase the monkeys. Swami Vivekananda acted accordingly and the monkeys fled away.'

The above is the reality of life. To overcome fear, a person has to face it outrightly. It is often observed that people who fly, despite the fear of flying become used to unfamiliar sensations associated with flying like, takeoff, turbulence etc. They get the opportunity to learn about what to expect during an air journey and get a chance to watch how others relax and enjoy an air ride. Gradually they can overcome the fear of flying.

All successful people attest to the fact that pushing through fear is less frightening than living with it. Directly facing fear with a well thought out action plan is the best way to respond to fear; it may cause some discomfort to start with but eventually will have an ending. The frustrations and discomforts a person may have to go through if he does not face his fear directly can be never ending.

19. PREPARATIONS TO FACE FEAR

To respond to fear, a person needs preparation. *Swami Sivananda* says, "*The only place where fear can exist, is your mind. It has no other residence.*" Fear always surfaces in the mind in the form of a thought; preparation to respond to fear therefore has to start in the mind.

More than 50,000 thoughts pass through the mind of a person every day. This means that almost every moment a person generates a thought which in other words means that every moment, there are opportunities for a person to impress his thoughts the way he desires. These opportunities can only be availed by those who monitor their thoughts and are ready to change them whenever they feel it is necessary.

It is not that successful people don't fear at all or avoid them; actually they interpret fear differently and address them accordingly. They change their thoughts, formulate plans and put them into actions before successfully responding to their perceived fear. Many people fail to overcome fear simply because of their inability to accept change and adapt to it. People in general develop a tendency to resist change because they overestimate the value of what they have and underestimate the value of what they may gain by giving it up; they are afraid of the unknown. It is not that some people have will power and some don't, the reality is some people are ready to change and the others are not.

Once a person decides to confront fear, it is prerequisite that he is aware of

- how long he has been affected by the thought of the particular fear.
- what triggers him the particular fear.

- how the fear influences his mind and behavior.
- why he wants to make a shift in his thinking.
- what he is going to do, and how his new thinking is going to help him to overcome the existing fear.

For every fear that a person has, there are certain things that drive or amplify it; all these drivers/amplifiers need to be identified. Against each driver/amplifier he/she then needs to find out:

- what is the worst that can happen.
- Whether he will be able to recover from the 'worst' and get on with the rest of his life.
- the strategy to be adapted to neutralize the possible adverse effect of each of the drivers/ amplifiers.

Through self talking, once a person identifies numbers of such drivers/amplifiers with associated strategies to neutralize the possible adverse effect of each driver (if any), he is better placed to clip the wings of the drivers/amplifiers and thereby reduce the strength of fear by eliminating the identified drivers/amplifiers one by one. Afterall every driver/amplifier contributes towards the fear and is responsible in making a person fearful, apprehensive or terrified about something.

While working out the worst that can happen against each driver/amplifier, it is generally observed that in majority of the cases of fear, the identified drivers/amplifiers are not threats to human life even though for some reason or reasons the 'Fight or Flight response' acts as if they are. Once the worst case scenario against identified drivers/amplifiers are worked out and are found to be of no threat to life, it gives a person the confidence that situations can only be improved from there and spurs him to prepare harder with strategies made to respond and diffuse the adverse effects of fear. ☙❧

20. DESENSITIZATION OF FEAR

The most essential ammunition a person can have to fight against fear is a strong desire from within. Confronting fear docs not always lead to a triumphant conclusion and immediate dissipation of the fear. In fact, in reality a person may have to confront his fear many times before he can declare it conquered. The person therefore has to have a strong motivation to patiently and persistently continue with his efforts and be prepared to accept failures if they surface on the way till his goal is achieved. A person with 'weak desire' often gives up his efforts to win over his fear on the slightest pretext of facing a setback. Such persons generally develop the tendency to equate setback with fate.

To overcome fear including phobia, different processes adapted are known as process of desensitization. Desensitization techniques can broadly be clubbed into the following classifications:

- Immediate exposure technique
- Gradual exposure technique
- Flooding technique
- Modeling technique

The same techniques may not be suitable for all types of fears. The effectiveness of any technique also depends to a large extent on the characteristics and attitudes of individuals adapting it; it therefore varies from person to person. In practice, a person has to try and find out which technique or combination of techniques suits him the most to deal with specific fear. Irrespective of whichever technique or combination of techniques a person adapts, he however must always be prepared to

- stand up for his actions even if it is a new step or a path that he had never taken or thought of in the past.
- take own responsibility and remain unmoved in the face of initial disappointments with the belief that things will ultimately get better even if they get worse to start with.
- stop at nothing till he can declare his fear as conquered.

Immediate exposure technique: It basically is a method through which a person directly confronts the things/ situations he fears. During execution, this technique has the potential to generate additional stress for a person since it is a direct and raw process. A person employing this technique therefore, must have the motivation and the will power to withstand the initial stress (if it occurs); he also must be mentally prepared to absorb the pressure of failed attempts (in case it happens). Without the above mental preparations, a bad or traumatic experience while employing this technique can push a person towards a situation where he will totally lose the desire to overcome his fear.

For an external fear, such as fear of a lizard (which is very common especially with the ladies), this technique warrants that a person either holds the lizard on his hand or allows it to crawl in his body. For an internal fear, such as fear of social interaction, this technique warrants that within a short span of time, a person gets exposed and involved in as many interactions with others as possible without losing interest to continue with the process further.

On the positive side, this technique enables a person to get out from the clutch of fear at the quickest possible time. If a person has the fear of rejection, and he is exposed to the situations he fears most and continues to get rejected, it will desensitize him to being rejected. Experience of rejection subsequently will have no impact on him. However, through this technique a person may have to try number of times before he can successfully overcome his fear.

Gradual exposure technique: In this technique a person exposes himself to the things/situations he fears in gradual and systematic steps. This process can be compared to the experience of a person in a swimming pool. In the pool, a person generally dips his toe first followed by other parts of the body and finally his whole body as his body gets progressively adjusted to the temperature of the pool water. For external fear, such as fear of a lizard, this technique warrants that a person over a period of time progressively

- thinks about a lizard.
- handles the picture of a lizard.
- sits in the same enclosure where there is a lizard.
- feels comfortable in his own way to stand close to a lizard.
- gathers courage to extend his hand close to the lizard.
- touches the lizard at least once.
- holds the lizard for a longer period of time and so forth.

In this technique the concerned person gets exposed to his fear in a relaxed way spread over a period of time till he summons up courage to eventually face it directly.

For internal fear, such as social interaction, a person can initially try interacting with a single person. On gaining in confidence he can make it a point to interact with a small social group without bothering about how he feels. With more and more of such exposures, as a natural process the person starts feeling comfortable with the group members. After gaining confidence, the person can try to participate in regular discussions with the group members. Over a period of time, these exposures will automatically make the person feel comfortable in social interactions with members of other groups too. This acquired confidence can eventually be extended to even public speaking by the person.

Flooding technique: When Nobel prize winning writer *Isaac Bashevis Singer* was resting at home after receiving the news of his award, a reporter appearing at his door asked him, *"Mr. Bashevis Singer, are you surprised? Are you happy?" "Of course, I am very surprised and happy"*, answered the elderly writer. After ten minutes, another reporter appeared and asked him, *"Mr. Bashevis Singer, are you surprised? Are you happy?"* the elderly writer replied, *"How long can a man remain surprised and happy?"*

The above is the rule of the life. Any emotion whether it is happiness or fear tends to fade over time. The principle of flooding is based on the above philosophy. Flooding involves prolonged exposure of a person to any situation or object he fears. It is a general observation that even very intense fear as a normal process loses its intensity and eventually subsides over a period of time. The flooding technique works both in real life fear as well as in imaginary fear. When the technique is utilized in imaginary fear, it is known as implosion.

Modeling technique: In this technique, a fearful person is encouraged to watch non fearful people confronting his events/ objects of fear with confidence and is made to replicate or imitate the same behavior towards his feared events/objects. This basically is a process of relearning by unlearning of the old knowledge. Most of the children get over their learned fear through application of this technique. Through this process a fearful person can get over his fear in a relaxed way spread over a period of time.

ઉ૪ઌ

21. ROLE OF BELIEF IN MANAGING FEAR

A person cannot feel fearful about a situation or an event unless he thinks and visualizes it as catastrophic or life threatening. It is only when a person starts taking things unduly seriously and gives more importance to them than they really deserve, fear starts dominating him. Belief plays a big role in dealing with fear. Without the belief that fear can be won over, a person cannot capitalize his knowledge about the fear and the specific technique to be applied to get over it. It is often seen that whenever a person with the belief of 'I can and I shall effectively deal with fear' puts his thinking, attention and efforts on his perceived fear, his subconscious mind starts knocking with ideas and insights and finally drives him towards achieving his objectives.

Belief and fear do not coexist. Simply stated, fear is unbelief or weak belief. As unbelief gains the upper hand in human thoughts, fear takes hold of the emotions. Belief is very powerful and is a pillar that supports all acts of creations and often makes a person free of worries and anxieties. It is rightly said, "*The beginning of anxiety is the end of faith, and the true faith is the end of anxiety*."

Belief or faith basically is a trust on something not necessarily based on proof. *Sri Sri Ravi Shankar* says, "*Faith is a wealth. It gives strength and stability.....If you lack faith you have to pray for faith.*" Yet to pray, you need faith. There are three types of faith according to him:

- **Faith in yourself:** Without faith in yourself, you think like, 'I cannot do this'/ 'This is not for me'/ 'I shall never feel freedom in my life'.

- **Faith in the world:** You must have faith in the world or you cannot move an inch.
- **Faith in divine power:** Have faith in divine and you will evolve.

He further said, *"All these faiths are connected. You must have all three for each to be strong. If you start doubting one, you are starting doubting everything."* Without faith, a person cannot focus on the course to victory in any journey.

Faith in oneself: Those who lack in trust on themselves often suffer from inferiority complex. They are constantly in fear of being rejected and disapproved by others. History reveals that there is no constraint in human mind, no walls around human spirit and no barrier to progress. All barriers to progress are manmade, they are created when thoughts of limitations (that arise out of fear) are allowed to make home in the mind. The feelings of inadequacy grow from the thoughts of fear. The best mental makeup to confront fear is to have the belief that it is surmountable and start doing things which a person once thought that he could not do. In spite of having pre apprehensions, people are often observed to carry out herculean tasks successfully. This only emphasizes the fact that human capability is stretchable; it needs only push through positive thinking, action and belief. Any fear, any obstacle is surmountable.

Faith in the world: The universe is controlled by the laws of nature. Everything in this world happens for a cause. Life does go through troughs and crests, and occasionally people do get hiccups but those times never continue indefinitely. People eventually find means to overcome whatever catastrophe happens in their life; so instead of being fearful, they should keep their eyes and ears open and fearlessly do the doables in time to make things happen in their life.

Faith in divine power: The tendency of regularly dwelling on perceived trouble creating situations and dangers should always be shunned, they often invite disasters. It has been an established observation that whatever a person constantly thinks and visualizes, it often materializes in reality.

In reality, there can be many more dangers in life of an individual than he ever anticipates. For example, a house collapse, or an accident by reckless and speedy car driving can totally shake up the rhythm of a person's life. It is not possible for any human being to identify and focus upon all possible dangers at all the times. The best decision is to do the doables against perceived and identified fears, and leave the rest to the Almighty with the mental preparation and alertness to deal with any eventuality when it surfaces. With limited vision, many people complain about the adversities which they encounter in life. They should always remember that things might have been worse if they were not protected by the divine power. It is rightly said,

"When we pray to Almighty,
He hears more than we say,
He answers more than we ask
And He gives more than we imagine
But He does everything in his own time and in his own way."

Human life and in fact the whole of the universe is governed by some divine laws. So, instead of dreading various untoward incidences that may appear in his life, a person should face them with preparations and positive frame of mind with the belief that

- nothing happens against God's will, and He does not approve anything that is not good for us.
- adversities never come without solutions. No problem eventually remains unsolved. ☙❧

Chaper Four

ANGER & ITS DIFFERENT FACES

A person almost always feels irritation, annoyance and so forth before his feelings eventually blossom into full fledged anger. The awareness of the 'blossoming' of anger that takes place in different stages therefore plays very important role in human life. Anger is a person's reaction to threat perception; it often floats on the emotion of fear. It embraces a person's

- *own self, self image or some parts of his identity*
- *loved ones*
- *properties and so forth*

Anger is always triggered by a stimulus which can either be internal or external, real or imagination based. Depending on how a person deals with it, anger can produce either positive or negative results. When a person is able to manage his anger well, it can lead him to make positive changes in his life as well as around him. Mismanaged, uncontrolled or misdirected anger on the other hand often–

- *lead to health problems, poor decision making and poor problem solving,*

- *create relationship problems with friends, relatives as well as colleagues at work.*

Nobody is born to express his anger in sets of specific patterns. All anger expressions are basically learned. Contrary to the perception of many that people can't control or change the way they react to anger, the reality is people can exercise control on their anger and change the way they respond to it. The above however necessitates thorough knowledge about anger in totality and willingness to adapt to changed thought process as per demand of circumstances. Awareness of different faces of anger and different techniques to neutralize their adverse effects help a person to face anger successfully.

22. THE ANGER PERCEPTION

Anger is a state of mind, prompted by happenings not liked by a person, resulting in impatience, irritability, disappointment, annoyance etc. A person almost always feels something else (primary feelings) first before he gets angry. That is why anger often is referred as secondary emotion. A person

- is said to be *impatient* when he struggles to check his immediate impulse in certain situation to say or do something to others in response of what they had done or said to him.
- gets *irritated* when he feels discomfort in the body and mind caused by reaction to an irritant (it can be anything that is said or done to him).
- gets *annoyed* when he does not like an object, an incidence, a circumstance, an action of others or even one of his own.
- feels *disappointed* when he finds that his hopes or expectations are not fulfilled because of certain events, circumstances, acts of others or even his own acts.
- feels *hurt* when he suffers pain mentally as well as physically arising out of others actions, deeds or comments towards him.
- feels *bitterness* (*resentment*) when he finds that others are opposing and coming in his way which otherwise would have enabled him to achieve something concrete.

- develops *hatred* towards something or someone when he dislikes them to the extent that he wants to cause harm to them in retaliation.
- expresses his *rage* (uncontrollable anger) when he is unable to cope with others 'obstructive attitude' towards him for a long stretch of time and eventually explodes.
- bears *grudge* towards others when he is unable to forgive others for their mistakes and he carries the feelings in his mind in order to cause harm to them.
- is said to be in a state of *revenge* mode when he develops the urge to do wrong to someone who has done wrong to him. He believes that he will get internal relief out of this act of retaliation.

All the above experiences arise out of a person's feelings of being either

- scared, humiliated, disrespected or rejected.
- attacked, offended or frustrated.
- forced, trapped or pressurized to accept something generally unacceptable to him under normal circumstances.

When the feelings of impatience, irritation, annoyance, hurt etc. as mentioned above become intense, they trigger the emotion of anger. This explains why like the tip of an iceberg, anger is visible while the impulse/impulses triggering it remains/remain underneath as shown in figure no. 13.

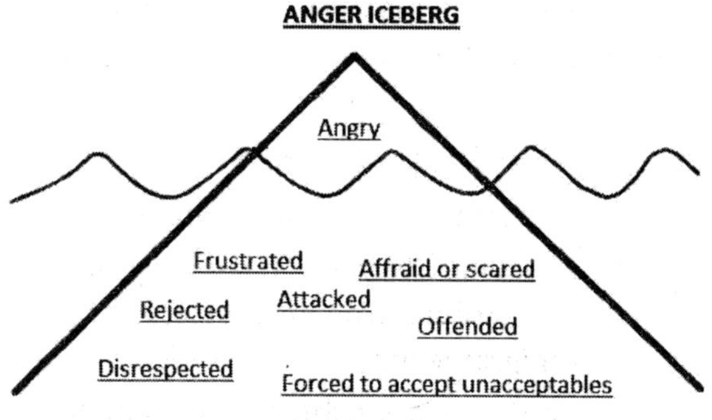

Figure no. 13.

Like fear, anger is always sparked by a stimulus which can either be real or imagination based. Under similar circumstances, the intensity of anger varies from person to person. The same person under similar circumstances can also feel different intensities of anger in different times.

Contrary to the perception of many people that only external factors like the insensitive actions of others, frustrating situations etc. trigger anger, the reality is, anger can be caused by both external as well as internal factors. While other persons, circumstances, events etc. are some of the external stimuli that trigger anger; memories, previous experiences, personal problems etc. are some of such internal stimuli that trigger anger. Some of the behavioural changes associated with anger are

- tension, frustration, reddened ears, teary eyes, crying,nose bleeding, shouting, inability to vocalize, bitterness, hurling insults, making threats and sarcastic remarks, destroying properties, objects, slapping others, avoidance, longer isolation, clenching of fists etc.

In fits of anger, a person's senses especially his thinking faculty gets distorted completely. Anger has the potential to lead a person to

- earn a bad reputation.
- create tension in the surrounding atmosphere.
- become a victim of health disorder in the form of cardiac problems, ulcers, blood pressure, migraine etc.
- poor relationships with family members, friends and colleagues.
- an isolated and secluded life.

23. CAUSES OF ANGER

Causes of anger can broadly be classified into two categories:

I. Direct

II. Subtle

Causes of Direct Anger

- Feeling of insult or humiliation
- Unfulfilled desire
- Disagreements
- Indifference of people
- Disrupted planning

Feeling of insult or humiliation: Anger is a natural feeling of a person whenever he is insulted (treated disdainfully or abusively) or humiliated (when made to feel ashamed or stupid in front of others). The feelings of insult or humiliation spring up in the mind of a person when he is snubbed by others either directly or indirectly.

Snubbing is an action or remark made scornfully by others and is directed towards a person with the intention to make him feel ignored or rejected.

Unfulfilled desire: It is said that anger is transmuted passion or desire. Whenever a person fails to gratify a burning desire or a passion, he loses his temper and gets angry on whomsoever or whatever he considers to be responsible for having come on the way to thwart his efforts in achieving his desired goal. Anger is directly proportional to desire. As strong the desire is as intense anger will be.

Disagreements: If people do not agree to the views of a person and instead opposes and criticises him, he gets angry.

Indifference of people: A person gets angry when people do not behave with him as per his expectations.

Disrupted Planning: A person gets angry when he fails to get a job done either because of his own short-comings or due to someone else's. He even gets angry when

- the situation gets out of his control like; natural disasters, Catastrophic situations, etc.
- he/she becomes unable to complete any work due to some external or internal hindrance.

Apart from the above, following factors also play an important role in making a person angry:

- When he sees a trait in others that he himself does not want to possess.
- When a current event brings to surface one of the old unresolved situation or disappointment or trauma that he had experienced in the past.
- When a person is stressed and his body resources are down.

The *subtle causes do not induce anger directly,* but they increase the vulnerability of a person to get angry under anger provoking situations. Following are some of the factors that subtly amplify anger:

- Loss of vital energy
- Increase in rajo-guna
- Disturbed state of mind arising out of fatigue, stress or poor health

Loss of vital energy: Reduced vitality makes people prone to irritability which eventually leads to the way to anger.

Regulated life to conserve vital energy (prana shakti) plays important role in anger management. The following have direct effect in regulation and conservation of vital energy:

- Physical activities
- Faculties of the mind
- Food habits

Physical activities: Large amount of vital energy gets consumed through digestion of food, pumping of blood by the heart to different organs in the body, sexual activities etc. Less sleep, excessive as well as uncontrolled sex, over eating etc. cause drainage of vital energy. Practice of pranayama helps in conservation of vital energy..

The faculties of the human mind: Human mind expend vital energy in emotion, thought, imagination etc. Emotional distress drains out vital energy like water from a tank. The more a person feels low or depressed, the weaker he becomes with reduced vitality.

Food habits: Maximum energy is expended by the body in the form of food digestion. Quality and quantity of food as well as frequency of eating therefore need to be very carefully regulated. Since vegetarian foods including milk are easily digestible compared to non-vegetarian food, they are preferred. Less vital energy is consumed in digesting them.

Increase in rajo guna: The human mind has three gunas or qualities born of nature - *satto, rajo* and *tamo*. In human beings, all the above three gunas exist in equilibrium with one of them playing the dominating role. At any moment, irrespective of whichever guna is dominant, an element of each of the balance two gunas always remain present in a person to maintain equilibrium. Prominence of gunas reflects on how people react to situations, make decisions and make choices to live their own life. Corresponding to the three gunas, there are three vrittis or modifications of the mind as mentioned below:

- Peace, equilibrium and balance come from *satto guna*.
- Anger manifests from *rajo guna*. A rajosik mind is restless and always tends to look for the defects in others and magnify their past errors and bad deeds.
- Carelessness, laziness and drowsiness come from *tamo guna*.

Rajo guna grows in a person primarily from

- food habits, like eating of spicy food, onion, garlic, coffee, tea etc.
- habit of excessive talking and arguing.
- reading of obscene and stimulating literature.
- watching of violent and obscene movies and so forth.

In a **disturbed state of mind arising out of fatigue, stress or poor health,** the tolerance level of a person against irritations and frustration of daily life gets diminished. He becomes prone to getting angry, sometimes even against a minor stimulus.

Under the above circumstances, some of the general and common situations in life which abet anger are: improper health condition or overwork, poor infrastructure, late running of trains, traffic jams, pollution -hot and humid atmosphere, overcrowded house, lack of training, funds, promotions, poor work culture, advance planning etc.

ଓଃ

24. MANIFESTATIONS OF ANGER

Anger manifests in many forms. While expressions of anger in some forms give advantage to a person in specific circumstances, there are expressions which can invite problems for him in the short term as well as in the long term. It is important to exercise control on expressions of anger. For general awareness, some of the manifestations of anger are discussed below:

I. **Verbal abuse**
II. **Constructive anger**
III. **Judgmental anger**
IV. **Overwhelmed anger**
V. **Deliberate anger**
VI. **Retaliatory anger**
VII. **Self inflicted anger**
VIII. **Shame based anger**
IX. **Habitual anger**
X. **Moral anger**
XI. **Sudden anger**
XII. **Displaced anger**
XIII. **Ignored anger**
XIV. **Chronic anger**
XV. **Egoistical anger**
XVI. **Addictive anger**
XVII. **Explosive or volatile anger**
XVIII. **Paranoid anger**
XIX. **Concealed anger**
XX. **Passive aggressive anger**
XXI. **Aggressive anger**
XXII. **Hate**

Verbal abuse is the outburst of anger which generally aims at frightening weaker people in order to get something done through them. It is expressed purely through words; no physical action is involved here. Verbal abuse is also directed towards criticizing and insulting a person against whom there are issues of complaints to be settled.

Constructive anger is healing by nature. It motivates a person to initiate actions especially in situations and circumstances that need a change for good. This type of anger often successfully leads a person to bring about positive reforms in different disciplines of life.

The intensity of constructive anger is often lower than its counterpart i.e. destructive anger. It can be effectively utilized only when a person is aware of the benefits of such type of anger.

A person with **Judgmental anger** is someone who often rushes to judgment without reason. By judgmental anger, a person generally tries to put other people down and make them feel low about themselves as well as their abilities. It is always directed towards others. It is also known as righteous anger. Depending on situations, it has the potential to add fuel to an otherwise ignited circumstance.

Overwhelmed anger is caused when circumstances become too hot for a person to cope with. It in fact occurs when overwhelming fear or a number of external demands or internal stressors overwhelm a person's coping ability; it is also known as flooded anger. It is often related to extreme case of frustration. A person generally experiences overwhelmed anger when he

- has a tight dead line ahead with lots of things to do.
- finds a job too demanding,
- struggles to raise children.

Deliberate anger is used by a person to gain power over a situation or any other person. Under normal circumstances, a person having such type of anger does not start out angry, he pretends to be angry to take care of those situations; eventually however he does get angry when things do not turn out the way he wants or someone tries to put spikes to some of his action plans.

Retaliatory anger is always directed towards an individual or an organization in order to 'get back at them' for a perceived wrong they have said or done. It is often caused by an insult, rejection or humiliation which eventually persuades a person to initiate revengeful action to settle issues. It is also known as pay back anger.

As the name suggests, **self-inflicted anger** is directed towards a person himself. It generally arises out of annoyance for failing on a task on hand or for being weak or incompetent in self assessment. Constantly turning angry feelings inward often lead a person towards disappointments and depressions. With self inflicted anger, people generally engage in self-destructive behaviors like overeating, starvation etc.

Shame based anger normally is person specific. Such angers are caused by a person's sense of internal state of inadequacy, unworthiness, dishonour or regret about which others may or may not be aware. People who need a lot of attention or are very sensitive to criticism often develop this style of anger. Slightest trigger of criticism sparks their anger instinct.

Habitually angry people generally are grumpy and they usually tend to get angry at small things that do not bother others. They may also go through their days looking for a fight and often tend to see the worst in everyone, and in every situation. These people are stuck in a pattern of behavior that over a period becomes dull; in spite of being predictable in nature such type of anger is very hard to change. Habitually angry persons need counseling to correct themselves.

People with **moral anger** always think that they have every right to be angry at others who have broken the 'rules'. They develop the belief that they are superior to everybody else and their anger is for a good cause. Seeing the world too simply, and failing to understand that people are actually different from the way they externally appear to be, are the basic characteristics of the morally angry people.

Sudden anger apparently zooms in from nowhere, blasts everything in sight, and then vanishes. It is generally experienced by a person when any of the following five 'S's or combinations of them figure prominently in his life.

- *Sleep deprivation* - this makes a person prone to irritation.
- *Stress at high level* - this makes a person more irritable and less resilient.
- *Sickness* - this reduces resilience and increases irritability of a person.
- *Substances* like alcohol - when ingested they dramatically intensify a person's emotions.
- *Sustenance* – warrants adequate and proper nutrition to a person. Intake of improper food, including junk food increases the likelihood of mood swings that affects the ability of a person to cope consistently with the next trigger that arises.

Displaced anger or **displacement anger** is the type of anger in which the angry person does not show his anger to the person or the object that infuriates him. Instead in most of the cases he shifts his attention and pours his anger on another person who comes across him and is considered by him as a safer target. Such situations

- often lead to soured relationships and
- do not permit the original anger to get resolved, it still continues to exist in the angry person with the potential to get built up over a period of time.

Ignored anger or **anger avoidance** are common with people who don't like to express anger much; they do not like even seeing other's getting angry. In spite of the fact that these people burn inside with anger, they dodge any expression of irritation by presenting a cool and happy face externally. Their misleading facial expression does not provide any opportunity to the offenders to make amends. Often the offenders apologize to such persons when realising that they have hurt other people.

Chronic anger is a condition in which a person becomes regularly upset or enraged over minor things. Negligence or verbal abuse in the childhood is perceived to be the prime factors that lead to the development of this type of anger. This type of anger can develop at different stages of a person's life. People with chronic anger issues face the risk of alienating close friends and loved ones, who find it uncomfortable or even frightening to be around them. Chronic anger is not at all desired, it puts stress on the immune system of a person and is closely linked to depression and other mood disorders.

Egoistical anger is a direct or indirect expression of anger characterized by acts of selfishness. People with this type of anger do not believe that rules exist to make life fair for all; they simply place self importance above everything. They believe in doing whatever pleases them; but if the outcome comes out to be negative, they get angry. They always try to deny their poor performance by threatening consequences to those who expose them.

As the name suggests, a person with **addictive anger** is literally addicted to it. He looks forward to the rush and excitement that addictive anger provides and tends to pick fights because he is always looking for an 'emotional high' even though he does not like the troubles this anger is often associated with.

When people express themselves in violent ways, it can be resulted as **explosive** or **volatile anger**. Volatile anger comes and goes; it often is quick, exaggerated and embarrassing to self as well as others. People with this type of anger can cause verbal or physical harm to others, object or even to themselves.

Paranoid anger springs up from unjustified feelings of suspicion and mistrust of others. This type of anger comes about when a person–

- feels jealousy towards others,
- feels that other people have or want to take what is rightfully his,
- acts out because he feels intimidated by others.

A person with **concealed anger** carries out secretive or indirect actions to get even with person who causes him the anger. This can involve sabotaging the other person's work by refusing to take messages, failing to notify another person about safety issues and purposefully damaging another person's work.

Passive aggressive anger can be described as a non-verbal aggression that manifests negative behavior. Individuals who employ a passive-aggressive interpersonal coping strategy generally avoid direct confrontations. It basically is a covert and active form of hostility. With passive anger, a person

- wittingly or unwittingly displays acts of sarcasm, apathy or meanness
- often participates in self-defeating behaviours such as alienating friends, family etc.
- performs poorly in professional or social circuits.

A person experiencing **aggressive anger** normally is aware of his emotion even if he does not understand the root cause of it. Aggressive anger often finds expression in the form of retaliation causing physical damage to properties or other people. Learning about different aspects of aggressive anger from his own experience as well as from the experiences of others helps a person to formulate effective strategies to deal with it.

Hate is hardened anger. It is a nasty anger style that happens when a person decides that the other person is totally wrong and is evil or bad. To forgive the other person is next to impossible for a hater; on the contrary, the hater vows to despise the offender. Hate starts as anger that does not get resolved. Hate is distinguished from anger in terms of intensity and duration. Hatred lasts longer and is more pervasive. It tends to overwhelm a person and obscure everything else he might feel; it persuades him to want to take action to hurt or destroy whatever inspired the hatred.

25. ROLE OF ANGER IN HUMAN LIFE

It is perfectly normal for a person to feel angry; the feeling isn't the problem—it's what he does with it that makes the difference. Contrary to the perception of many people who consider anger as bad and treat it as though it is unreasonable and unmentionable, it is to be noted that like all other emotions, anger too has its purpose which can be used to good effects. Anger has the potential to persuade a person to

- mobilize resources to achieve something concrete.
- act on his sense of justice.
- get quick results in demanding situations.
- take control of certain situation.
- become assertive.

It is a common observation that in a state of anger a person generally is capable of completing most of the tasks that he has on hand.

Mobilization of resources to achieve something concrete: Anger has the potential to

- agitate a person who normally feels helpless and incompetent to deal with the challenges of life, and make him feel empowered by competence and confidence to stand up straight to the conflicts and frustrations which he had been avoiding for long.
- persuade a person to accept the anger impulse as the source of inspiration to mobilize resources, strategise action plans and implement them on priority to achieve something concrete.

Under the above circumstances, anger plays the role of an activating and mobilizing force.

Acting on the sense of justice: Anger has the potential to provide the motivation to a person to

- constructively correct an injustice and urge him to act on his sense of justice.
- fight against oppression and topple a tyrant.

In the above context it is worthwhile to mention that anger caused the initiation of actions that eventually eliminated 'slavery' and 'apartheid'.

Getting quick results in demanding situations: By showing anger, as opposed to remaining calm and pleasant, in certain situations, a person can get extra outputs from others in the form of quick results. This is because many people by nature when intimidated by an angry person often become more obliging than they are under normal circumstances.

The above philosophy however does not work on blunt expression of anger in all circumstances. This is mainly because there are also people who do not respect a person who does not control his anger or hold opposing viewpoints all the time. They are more willing to listen to a person and accommodate his needs if he communicates in a respectful way. Keeping the above in view, a person needs to inculcate the habit of expressing his anger appropriately without being verbally or physically abusive.

Take control of certain situation: Anger makes a person feel powerful; depending on circumstances, it often enables him to express himself forcefully and take full control of typical situations. Such instances however are case specific.

Become assertive: Anger under specific circumstances gives confidence and courage to a person to stand up against others for a cause. This is an act of assertiveness and that make others respect the angry person. Assertiveness can be explained as a style of communication in which a person is able to express his feelings, thoughts, beliefs, and opinions in an open manner that doesn't violate the rights of others.

On the negative side, anger activates the human stress mechanism which causes the Fight or Flight response. When this response continues for a long time or occurs frequently, it has damaging affect on a person in the form of poor physical health and imbalanced mental functioning.

Anger when unmanaged has the negative potential to cause

- erosion of a person's interpersonal as well as work related relationships.
- a person to behave aggressively and violently.
- anger to others.

Anger can affect physical health: Anger activates the human stress mechanism which in turn activates the sympathetic nervous system and the medulla gland system causing the body to respond with fight or flight response. This response is life-saving under normal circumstances. However, if it persists for a long stretch of time or occurs frequently, it can cause headache, migraines, chest pain etc, while in the long term perspective it can complicate the existing health conditions in the form of problems with cardiovascular systems, muscles and joints, body's immune systems, endocrine systems, respiratory systems, skins, gastro-intestinal system and so forth.

Anger can affect mental functioning: Repetitive bouts of anger can consume huge amounts of mental energy and cloud a person's thinking capacity. Anger bypasses the rational mind of a person where more thought out beliefs exist. It also makes his thinking distorted. As a result, his judgment gets impaired and he often fails to see the broader perspective of life.

Anger erodes interpersonal as well as work related relationships : An angry person often loses his temper and starts doing or saying things which he would not usually contemplate. Constructive criticism, creative differences, heated discussions and debates arising out of anger can always be healthy, but out of anger when a person lashes out at others, he loses their support and sympathy. Once, a person earns the reputation of being aggressive or violent, it follows him wherever he goes. People find it very difficult to trust such persons and are not comfortable to frankly discuss any issue with them. This is simply because people never know what is going to set them off or what they are going to do.

Anger angers others: The impact of anger on others is two-fold:

- the sheer force of the anger that assaults it's recipient.
- the accumulative impact, where the recipient stores the anger in their body.

Although the impact of anger is immediately apparent in one-on-one exchanges, the accumulative anger often causes more damages to the person who has been angered by the angry person. In the latter case, anger gradually builds up inside and eventually explodes on a minor trigger. Incremental accumulations of anger are really very difficult to detect.

People in general use anger as a self defense. Without looking at it rationally, its frequent use as self-defense however has the potential to stall human progress. It is relevant in this context to quote ace Indian tennis player *Sania Mirza.* While being interviewed by a sports journalist of The Telegraph, Kolkata, on 25th November 2015, she said, *"I am aware of my minuses.*

One big minus is that I use anger as a form of defense. As I have matured, I have been able to curb that."

Anger has the potential to turn a person into its slave. It is relevant to quote the following anecdote in this context. *While leaving India after his conquest, Alexander the Great recalled that he was asked by his people to carry a yogi with him. He spotted a yogi in deep meditation in a secluded place. Once the yogi got up from his meditation, Alexander went close to him and proposed him to accompany him to Greece where he would be provided everything including accommodation in his palatial building. When the yogi refused to accept his offer, Alexander felt insulted; shaking in anger, he reminded the yogi that he was the conqueror of the world and unfurling his sword menacingly threatened the yogi with dire consequences if he did not accept his proposal. The yogi smiled and drawing Alexander closer to him replied firm but politely, "You have made two statements just now. Both are invalid statements. First you cannot cut me to pieces. You can only cut my physical body but not me. I am immortal, deathless and eternal. Secondly, though you claim to be the conqueror of the world, to me you are the slave of my slave." Alexander stood listening, speechless. The yogi continued, "Anger is my slave and you are slave of anger. See how easily you lose your temper! Does not that make you a slave of my save?" The world conqueror then realized that all his conquests were in vain until he managed to conquer the anger that lay within.* This is the reality of life.

26. ANGER REGULATION

The common approaches to address anger are

- Suppressing
- Expressing
- Calming

When a person is angered by a situation, event or another person and does not express his annoyance for reasons best known to him, his feelings remain *suppressed* within. These feelings find expressions later but often in a distorted way. In most of the cases of suppressed anger, the angry person suffers more than the person who was the cause of his anger. In many cases, the anger causing person even remains unaware that he was the cause of the anger. The angry person however is always aware of whosoever caused the anger.

Suppression of anger affects the free flow of energy within the body of a person. This eventually leads to its build up in the form of blocked energy with potential to cause severe health problem in future. Through suppression, a person does not get rid of his anger; he simply pushes it to the subconscious mind where it accumulates till it finds expression often with multiplied adverse effects.

There are people who have tendency to suppress and then convert and redirect their anger. They hold the anger inside, divert attention to something positive and stop thinking about it. Their aim is to inhibit or suppress anger and convert them into more constructive behaviour later. The problem with this type of response is that whenever the anger expression is restricted, it turns inward and finally leads to hypertension, high blood pressure or depression.

While suppression of anger is unhealthy, expressing it with an aggressive outburst (without self analysis) is no better. Both have the potential to fuel the fire and reinforce the anger problem. Expression of anger in a hostile and aggressive manner puts others in the defensive and exacerbates the situation further; it often leads to ruined relationships both at personal as well as at professional level.

The best way to express anger is to do it *assertively.* Assertiveness is a style of communication in which a person even in a state of anger expresses his feelings, thoughts, beliefs, and opinions in an open manner without intruding into the rights of others. Words, tone of the voice and the body language used in assertive expression is distinctly different from that of aggressive expression of anger.

It however has to be kept in mind that assertive expression is simply a style of communication; it does not give guarantee to a person that by adapting it he is going to get whatever he wants under all circumstances. Depending on circumstances, a person even with assertive expression may sometimes have to settle for a mutually accepted compromise. Understanding assertive style of expression provides an option to a person to make a choice as to when he should be assertive. In the field of psychology and psychotherapy, assertiveness is a learnable skill and mode of communication.

The function of anger in human body can be compared to the function of a safety valve in a boiler. When pressure within the boiler builds up and reaches a pre-determined level, the safety valve auto releases the pressure within by discharging steam before it reaches the critical level. In similar way, anger acts as a devise in the human body to let internal pressure off before it accumulates to a critical level of explosion. Anger determines the tolerance level of a person; it measures how much pressure his psyche can tolerate before it literally explodes. It serves a useful purpose in releasing pent-up energy, the accumulation of which over a period of time can cause lots of harm to human body.

Like the operation of boiler needs to be regulated with proper attention to ensure that it does not reach the critical level, every emotional attack of anger needs to be very carefully dealt with so that internal pressure is not allowed to keep on accumulating and build up to a critical level.

The level of tolerance of anger varies from person to person. If the incidences of minor irritation or annoyance are kept suppressed and accumulated for a prolonged period, generally a time comes in the life of a person when there will be no space left for him to accommodate any more irritation. During such periods, even a minor stimulus can cause explosion and lead him to throw tantrums and blow things out of proportion.

In view of above, the emotion of anger needs to be regulated at a lower level of tolerance with lots of introspection and thoughtful considerations at every stage. The above necessitates that a person is conversant with the different stages through which anger blossoms (refer section 27 of chapter four).

It is observed that people in general have no control over everything happening in this world but they certainly can exercise control over their reactions to what happens.

Awareness of the following enables a person to formulate and implement strategies to control his anger and thereby improve his tolerance level against it:

- Different types of anger expressions
- Causes of the occurrences of different types of anger
- Introspection of the anger characteristics of self as well close associates
- Calming of the mind through numbers of techniques discussed in section 28 of chapter four.

☙❧

27. HOW ANGER BLOSSOMS?

Psychologists have identified the following seven different stages through which mild irritation caused by a stimulus increases in intensity and peaks as rage:

First stage: Mild irritation/annoyance etc. generally is the starting point of any anger. Most of the people on daily basis dwell on this stage. This stage is commonly known as the stage of activation of anger. At this stage, when irked by an everyday incident, a person generally keeps things simple. He continues to be rational enough to realize that

- though the incident tickles him, it is relatively unimportant and
- if he bothers too much about it and makes a big deal out of it, others will consider him to be a lunatic.

Second stage: At this stage, commonly known as the '*stage of deliberation*', where a person's thought process plays an active role; he tries to analyze and bring into light reasons of irritations. At this stage, facts are analyzed, opinions are formed and complex results of actions or events are sought.

Mild irritation doesn't progress beyond this point, and people who use anger as a constructive outlet for clearer communication, rarely move any further from this stage.

Third stage: At this stage, a person starts feeling tensed that causes to escalate slight provocation. Following symptoms are apparent in a person at this stage:

- Change in the voice tone
- Change in facial expression with sign of annoyance
- Change in body language with more aggressive posturing

The anger at this stage almost comes up to the surface showing signs of eruption. Much of the expression however still remains inward and ordinal. This stage is known as the '*stage of escalation*'.

The fourth stage: This stage is the turning point that determines if a person will remain just irritated or annoyed or shift onward and become truly angry. A person's grip on reality is likely to shift to slipping mode from this stage.

In this stage objectivity often gets lost and reason for a course of action is fabricated to justify the angry outburst even if it bears little resemblance to reality. This stage is also known as the '*stage of confabulation*'.

Fifth stage: The main expression of anger really begins at this stage. All expressions of anger are thrust outward at this level often with exaggerated behaviour to attract attention. Since a person gets instigated and incited at this level, this stage is known as the *'stage of instigation'*.

Sixth stage: At this stage a person is on the brink of a disaster; he is confused and fearful. Since this is a stage of anxiety or dismay, it is also known as '*stage of consternation*'. If careful attention is paid, from this stage most of the people can return back to their lower and less agitated states. This stage is considered to be an emotional stop-valve before a person reaches the dangerous 'action stage of anger'.

Seventh stage: At this stage a person is ready to confront the source that causes him anger. Here the anger converts from an emotional state into an aggressive behavior that seeks physical expression. Not every action at this stage results in violence, but the intensity of rage is so explosive and the loss of control so blinding, that the possibility of its outburst cannot be ruled out. Since this stage is associated with the intention of a person to 'destroy', it is also known as the *'stage of destruction'*.

The first four stages of development of anger can be called the thought stage. Between fifth and sixth stage thoughts generally get transformed to speeches. The movement from sixth to seventh stage is called the action stage.

Anger can be controlled with relative ease at the thought stage, failing which a person should attempt to control it in the speech stage. In this context it is relevant to narrate the following incident which reveals interesting learning.

A couple with their daughter was having breakfast in a table. The daughter accidently knocked a coffee cup and splashed coffee in the father's shirt. This caused the following chain reactions:

- The father cursed and scolded his daughter; turning towards his wife, he then criticized her for placing the cup close to the edge of the table. This led into a verbal dual between them.
- Infuriated, the father went upstairs and changed his shirt. Coming down, he found his daughter still crying. He could not get the daughter ready in time to catch the school bus which left in time. The mother also left for her work in time.
- The father along with daughter subsequently rushed to his car. Being late, the father drove faster than he normally does. On the way, for over speeding, the father had to pay a penalty to the traffic police. Finally they reached the school but not in time.

- Being late, the daughter got down from the car and ran straight towards the school without saying good bye to the father.
- Reaching office 30 minutes late, the father realized that he had forgotten to bring his brief case. The father obviously was very upset. He was looking for returning home early. When he finally returned home, he could feel a small wedge in his relationship with his wife and daughter.

In the above particular case, the father had the option to diffuse the situation by controlling his anger either in the 'thought development stage' or in the 'speech development stage' as mentioned below:

In the 'thought development' stage, as the coffee splashed over his shirt and he saw the daughter about to cry, the father could have diffused the situation by politely consoling her daughter to be more careful in future instead of rebuking her. He then could have gone upstairs and come back after getting ready and collecting his briefcase as usual.

Even after feeling that anger has set in, in the 'speech development' stage, the father could have remained silent, gone upstairs, changed his shirts and got down in time after collecting his brief case and see off his wife and daughter to their respective vehicles.

It is possible for a person to nip anger in the bud at the thought development stage itself by developing the skills to cleanse his mind of angry thoughts and replacing them with more harmonious thoughts. These skills can be developed through practice of various techniques referred in section 28 of chapter four.

However, once the thought development stage is over and anger is formed, it dominates the mind and threatens to enter the speech stage. At the speech stage, the wisest decision is to refrain from uttering any words by maintaining silence so that things are kept under control. Expressions of anger through uncontrolled speech often add fuel to other person's fury. During this stage, remembering the old adage that damage caused to others by words uttered take longer time to heal encourages and inspires a person to maintain his silence. It is relevant to quote the following old adage in this context:

"A Wound from an arrow will heal in time,
The chopped tree could sprout again in time,
An unpleasant word uttered when lodged in ears,
Inflicts a mortal wound not be healed in years."

When anger crosses the speech stage, it enters the dangerous 'action stage' where it can take a violent shape unless checked. In this stage people generally lose control on their reasoning faculty and often inflict miseries not only on them but also on people around them. Here conscious application of anger management techniques (refer section 28 of chapter four) helps a person to control his anger to a great extent. At this stage, even lying down on the bed (when not sleeping) helps in exercising control over anger. No violence generally erupts in a person when he is lying down.

With the awareness of the causes of anger, various stages of anger, types of anger, role of anger in human life and his own anger characteristics, a person is better placed to introspect and identify strategies to deal appropriately with anger. There are various techniques (immediate, short term as well as long term) through which strategies can be formulated to manage and keep anger at bay. These techniques are discussed in section 28 of chapter four.

☙❧

28. STRATEGIES TO DEAL WITH ANGER

It is relevant to quote *Swami Vivekananda* in the context of anger. He said, *"We waste two thirds of our energy in useless emotions such as anger".* If a person can utilize even a fraction of this untapped energy, all his dreams and projects would then be within his reach. Every individual therefore should strive hard to curb his anger.

When anger is triggered, every individual reacts in a specific way as per his habit or style. Nobody is born to express his anger in sets of specific patterns. Anger expressions are mostly learned. Contrary to the perception of many that people can't change the way they react to anger, the reality is, people can change the way they express or deal with their anger.

In a situation of conflict, a person cannot change others, the only thing he can do is change his reactions to what makes him angry; this enables him to handle any conflict that may arise, without letting the situation to slip out of control. When angry, there are essentially *three basic ways to interrupt a behavioral pattern* as mentioned below. They all have positive and immediate impact on circumstances:

- (i) Visual – Changing of thoughts
- (ii) Verbal – Changing of language used
- (iii) Kinesthetic – Changing of physical postures

The awareness that anger is setting in or have set in is the key factor in determining what is to be done next in order to clip the possible destructive wings of anger. Knowledge about the various causes of anger, different types of anger and a person's own patterns of anger play big roles during his introspection to prepare for combating it. Anger management basically is a procedure of acquiring the skills to recognize the signs that a person is becoming angry, and taking action to deal with the situation in a positive way. In no way anger management means holding the anger in or trying to keep from feeling angry. Effective dealing with anger embraces the following steps:

- Identification of the source causing the anger
- Thinking of potential solutions before responding
- Considerations of the consequences of each solution
- Making a decision by picking up an option or assimilating parts of different options
- Checking progress i.e. follow up

To deal effectively with anger and keep it at bay, various techniques can be adapted. These techniques are broadly clubbed into three categories:

- Immediate measure
- Short-term measure
- Long- term measure

The basic idea of the above techniques is 'cooling down'; this helps in burning up the spurt of emotional energy associated with anger. Once that energy is spent, anger gradually subsides.

Immediate measures to deal with anger: Following are some examples of immediate measures which can be adapted to effectively deal with anger.

- ***Counting numbers aloud or even whispering them within:*** Counting numbers from 0 to 10 or up to 20 helps a person to pacify anger. Sometimes counting backward from 50 or even from 100 gives instant relief to a person and helps him to cool down and to deal with anger more rationally.

- ***Getting away to regain composure:*** Sometimes flight is better than fight. Getting away i.e. taking a break from the anger provoking atmosphere or circumstance helps a person to cool down and think things through. Taking few minutes of mindful walk to get some fresh air or even slowly drinking a glass of water enables a person to get uncoupled from the ongoing thought of anger and thereby release his pent-up energy within. After cooling off, the person can re-group and re-assess his thoughts. The above practice is especially helpful when a person feels that the pressure of stress arising out of anger is escalating within and is going out of control.
- ***Taking mental escape:*** When stuck up with the thoughts of anger, diverting the attention to something of choice, like listening to music or singing at the top of the voice can provide relaxation to the otherwise aroused mind of a person. With composure reassured, the thinking faculty works sharper. As a result, a person about to shout and scream, can resort to only few chosen words and thereby take control of a typical situation.
- ***Deep breathing eases the tension associated with anger:*** Deep breathing (refer abdominal breathing in chapter two) helps in counteracting tension and lowering of the internal anger meter. Few rounds of long breaths enable a person to bring peace and calmness to his mind, and the attended sharpening of his thinking faculty helps him in making rational decisions.

- ***Consciously forcing the mind and body to relax:*** Providing relaxation to the specific muscles of the hands, arms, shoulders, neck etc. in the form of asanas, a person can ensure dissipation of anger in a big way (refer chapter two).
- ***Lowering of raised voice:*** Consciously lowering the voice after realizing that he is shouting out of anger enables a person in a state of anger to exercise control on his emotion in the form of usage of proper language. Language is very powerful and has its influencing effect on the subconscious mind. In the state of anger, negative words like don't, not, no, can't etc. should always be replaced by words of opposite meaning, because human mind do not understand the difference between negation and affirmation, it simply follows the command.

Short term measures to deal with fear: Following are examples of some short term measures to deal with anger:

- ***Conscious development of will not to get angry:*** When a person gets angry, he may or may not harm the person he is angry with, but he definitely harms himself. *The Gita* says, *'Man is his own friend and man is his own enemy'*. When a person succumbs to anger, he becomes his own enemy. Effective use of will power enables a person to exercise control over his anger if necessary by even adapting to a changed thought process. The following incident is very relevant in this context.-

There was a very ill tempered boy who often used to lose his temper even over small issues. After sometime people were surprised to notice that he had been able to tame his anger outbursts. On being asked how he could bring about such a big change in him, he replied, *"Every morning when I wake up from sleep, I say to myself that I have two choices before me - to be angry or not to be angry. I choose the latter. Throughout the day I keep on reminding myself that I must remain true to my choice. Come what may, I must not lose my temper, at least for this particular day. People may not treat me properly, things may not turn out the way I want them to, but this one day I must never be angry. I may be angry tomorrow, but surely not today."*

With will power and conscious thinking, a person can even maintain silence when he perceives that a thought of anger has been developing within him. He thereby can control his anger in the speech stage before things go out of the hand and moves to the action stage.

- ***Better Communication:*** When a person is angry, his emotion generally takes centre stage and inhibits his ability to cool down and pause. Pausing and cooling down has the potential to take a person beyond reacting into a more subtle and balanced state of responding. It makes him feel feet on the ground and air on the skin. Reactions are always instinctive, whereas responses are backed by thoughtful consideration. Unlike reacting where a person normally acts on impulse and brings in more of complication to the situation, while responding a person gets time to slow down, take time to think and evaluate carefully about what to say. He is also able to make appropriate choice of words, body language and expression to ensure that his response does not create any adverse impact.

In states of anger, direct and verbal communication after finding the suitable time of interaction always yields better results. Text messages, letters, emails etc. are to be avoided since they are often misinterpreted. When a person realises that he is 'wrong', it is always a wise decision to communicate his feelings to the opposing person/persons. This helps in diffusing many otherwise volatile situations.

- ***Diffusing situations:*** Angry people generally tend to demand things - be it fairness, appreciation, agreement, or doing things their way. In the process they further aggravate situations. Every person gets hurt, disappointed or frustrated whenever he does not get what he wants. Under such circumstances how he puts up his wishes to others is more important. When a person says that he likes to have something rather than saying that he must have it, it can help him to diffuse rather than flare up many otherwise complicated situations.
- ***Usage of logic:*** In state of anger, it is important for a person to think and use logic. It is always to be remembered that the world is not out to get at any specific person and that every individual experiences anger as one of life's inevitable rough spots. When angry, this belief will enable a person to be more rational and get a more balanced perspective. It is relevant to quote *Sri Sri Ravi Shankar* in this context. He said, *"It is not people who hurt you. It is your foolishness, your own mind, your own vulnerability and your own emotions that entangle you, and make you feel hurt. Do you think people have no other business that they want to come and hurt you? Do they get a lottery by hurting you? Wake up and see, is there an intention in them to hurt you? You need to see things from other side*

as well. ... Many times it so happens that you never intended to hurt someone, yet they felt hurt by your action. What do you tell these people who feel that you have hurt them? You say, 'I did not mean it, something happened through me. I did not mean to hurt you, but an incident or event happened that gave you an idea that I hurt you."

- ***Forgiveness helps in resolving anger:*** Unable to forgive someone is like drinking poison and expecting the other person to die. Resolution lies in releasing the urge to punish. The longer a person holds on to anger, the more painful emotions he will experience, the more turbulence he is putting in his body, the more damage he inflicts on his long-term health and wellness. It is worth mentioning an anecdote in this context. One day while Lord Buddha was sitting underneath a tree in a village with his disciples, an angry and excited man spat on his face. Lord Buddha just wiped his face with a piece of paper and continued to talk. Meanwhile the angry man realized his folly and out of his repentance was looking for the master to go to him and apologize for his act out of anger. He could not find the master in the same place but after gathering information from others could trace the master the next day sitting under a tree with numbers of disciples in another village. Seeking apology, he fell on the feet of the master. The master could not recognize the man. But when he was reminded by the man what he did to him and why he was apologizing, the master said, "Is this the same village, the same tree or the same people? Is this even the same time? What is past is gone. Why do you carry yesterday into today? I left yesterday then and there. I never accepted what you did, but instead sent love to you." This is compassion.

Grudges are not to be nursed. A grudge is the only thing that does not get better when it is nursed.

- ***Getting self relief:*** It becomes easier for a person to forget about an anger episode that constantly tickles him when he offloads it from the mind. The method of offloading adapted can vary from person to person. The following anecdote is relevant in this context. A person once approached *Abraham Lincoln* and asked for his suggestion saying that he has been hurt by the repeated taunting of one of his friends. He further said that in spite of his best of efforts, he is unable to forget the hurt; it haunts him every moment. Lincoln suggested, "Why don't you write a letter to him, telling him everything you hold in your mind against him? Write as harshly as you can. The man drafted a letter accordingly and returning to Lincoln said, "I have written the letter as advised by you. May I now post it to him?" "Now, just tear it up and throw the pieces into the fire and forget all about it" replied Lincoln.

Lincoln's suggestion carries a message within – *offloading of the feelings of irritation from within relieves a person internally.*

Long term measures to deal with anger: Usage of humourous imagery is an efficient tool in anger management. Laughing off the anger issue just like that however can be self defeating, since this ignores the basic issue at hand. Some of the examples of long term measures to keep anger at bay are:

- ***Practice of meditation*** – discussed in section 14 of chapter two and practice of pranayamas – discussed in section 13 of chapter two
- ***Balancing of gunas with food habits*** – discussed in section 23 of chapter four.
- ***Preservation of vital energy with disciplined life*** - as discussed in chapter two, practice of pranayama and listing of all that angers a person with efforts to solve them in advance.
- ***Study of human reactions patterns particularly against anger*** – a part of it has been discussed in section 24 of chapter four.
- ***Introspection*** to identify self short comings and agreeing to others' good habits.
- ***Listening*** to lectures of spiritual teachers.

When angry, a person needs to keep in mind

- never to go in an argument with a person who angers him.
- to avoid anything that will escalate anger, like watching violent movies or T.V shows.
- not to dwell on the past incidences of anger and their consequences no matter what they were.

Unless a person has control on his own anger, he will not have the mental clarity to deal with the anger of others. Practicing different anger pacifying techniques in order to gain control over anger therefore is very important. While facing an angry person, the knowledge of the following helps a person to deal with him appropriately:

- Argument and counter argument with an angry person will never yield positive result, on the contrary it is likely to fuel his anger further and escalate the situation. This is mainly because most of the angry people have insecurity issues that they cover up with an angry façade and also during the state of anger, their mental faculty do not work rationally.

- What an angry person says, is hardly factual but emotional in content, related to his fear, frustration and bruised ego. When an angry person shouts, it is better to keep silent or speak slowly and calmly with lowered vocal tone and non-threatening body language; when he says a lot, it is better to say nothing or say very little. This will often encourage the angry person to calm down.
- Constantly trying to appease the anger of an angry person or accepting blame for how he feels always need to be avoided, since this is likely to make him feel that anger is an effective tool to get what he wants.
- Going to his close proximity and hugging an angry person always need to be avoided since in a state of arousal, he can turn out to be violent any time.
- Suggesting different methodologies to an angry person in order to help him to cool down his mind always need to be avoided till his steam is off to quite an extent since this has the potential to flame his anger even more because in the state of anger he often feels that his emotions are being ignored.
- Once the angry person's steam is off, he can be talked to in order to find out the cause of his anger and also with whom or with what he is angry and also how his anger can be resolved.

VITAL ENERGY OR PRANA OR PRANA SHAKTI REFERRED IN SECTION 23 OF CHAPTER FOUR

For sustenance of human life, the following external resources are essential:

- Continuous supply of oxygen from air
- Periodical nourishments through supply of foods and liquids (such as water, fruit juice etc)
- Exposure to sun rays

Even if a person falls sick to the extent that he cannot:

- breathe properly to inhale air (oxygen), he can be given the input through external support.
- gulp food of his own, he can be fed externally.
- take in any liquid of his own, he can be provided external support for liquid intake.
- move of his own, he can be moved through external supports and exposed to sun rays.

But the moment the person is declared dead, immediately all his mental and physical activities (including the act of breathing) stop permanently. The above leads to the perception that there is an element whose presence in the body keeps it alive with all the organs of the body functioning. The moment this element leaves the body, all the organs of the body becomes nonfunctional and the body is declared dead. This element in Indian scriptures is called prana, in China they call it 'qi' and in Japan they call it 'ki'. Prana, also known as the vital energy or the prana shakti is a divine energy and is derived from the cosmic prana also known as universal prana or universal consciousness or cosmic consciousness or universal chaitanya. Prana is a vibratory energy that is omnipresent in the universe. It is perceived since time immemorial that this divine energy–

- transcends the time and space.
- influences the life and health of living beings.
- impregnates, structures and sustains all the animate as well as inanimate objects in this universe.

Every form that exists and can be seen or sensed like air, liquids, solids, sun moon, stars, human or animal body, plants etc. are creations of cosmic prana. It is all pervading, and is so subtle that it is beyond ordinary perception. It is seen only when it becomes gross and takes a form.

Human being is born through prana and lives by it. Prana is a sanskrit word constructed of the syllables 'pra' and 'an'. 'An' means movement and 'pra' is a prefix meaning constant. Prana therefore means constant motion. This constant motion as per yogic philosophy commences in the human being as soon as a person is conceived in his mother's womb. Subsequently, as the body formation takes place and a baby comes on earth, he goes on drawing prana from the cosmic prana on regular basis during the entire period of his life.

Prana is a type of energy responsible for the body's life, heat and maintenance. It is similar to electricity in that it is not physically seen but supplies an invisible current that keeps life flowing and functioning. It is the prime mover of all the activities starting from gross physical movement to minute biochemical processes in the human body. Prana is indestructible; it can take the form of any matter or energy. With regulated life style, food habits and practice of pranayama expenditure of prana, the vital energy from the human body can be controlled.

READERS' COMMENTS ABOUT TARIT KUMAR PAL'S OTHER BOOKS PUBLISHED FROM THE HOUSE OF M/S PUSTAK MAHAL', NEW DELHI

POWER OF THOUGHTS:
FIRST EDITION: LATE AUGUST 2013
SECOND EDITION: MAY 2014.

- Heartiest congratulation on writing such an enlightening narrative....I would ask my colleagues from Learning department to do a book reading session on your book with associates. C.P.Gurnani, CEO Mahindra Satyam and Managing Director Tech Mahindra.
- The book is a very interesting read. Topics are covered in excellent order and many anecdotal examples are from real life Indian situations making it easier to relate to. We all have some knowledge on the topics taken up; the book converts this knowledge into understanding well Sanjiv Agarwal, Managing Director, MJR Steels, Kolkata.
- I just completed reading your wonderful book. It is simply superb................I feel it must be read and reread and suggest friends to procure and read. Gopikanta Ghosh. Author and former Joint Chief Executive Officer, Khadi and Village industries Commission, Mumbai.
- "Many deviate from their path for lack of determination under pressure of unfavorable circumstances. Author has given many examples and also from his long executive career stressed the importance and impact of positive thoughts in building up successful career. A must read for

all youths to build up strong thought process. This book will also help young executives in their decision making." Dr.S.K Dutta Choudhury, Rtd. Director. West Bengal Health Services.

- The book is so much simpler and generalized that it will have wide spectrum of customers. I am sure it will be super hit and one of the best selling books. Prof. Dr. S.K. Patel, Deptt. of Mech. Engg. National Institute of Technology, Rourkela.
- POWER OF THOUGHTS written by Mr. Tarit Kumar Pal from the personal experience is a step by step guide to develop positive attitude. Rati Kanta Ghosh, Managing Director, Effluent & Water Treatment Engineers (P) Ltd, Kolkata.
- . ... The book is excellent. Though I have gone thru it once, but I have to go through many times in order to get to the core. The book is not meant only for budding managers but also for people of all walks of life and all cross section of the society, even for homemakers. C.Tarafdar, Rtd. From M/s Voltas, Patna
- We had bought 40 copies of your book from Pustak Mahal and presented to all General Managers and ED's of DSP. I enjoyed reading your book and found it very compelling. We are planning to buy another 100 copies for giving to our Management Trainees. Mrs. Reeta Banerjee, G.M (HRD) DSP, Durgapur, SAIL. (Durgapur Steel Plant bought 101 copies more subsequently).
- The book Power of thoughts has been distributed among Sr. Officials of NMDC i.e GM and above. Overall response has been good and few officials

told that the book is worth reading and useful for managers.................Srinivasa Rao. NMDC Limited, Hyderabad.

- Power of thoughts is a matured offering .Managing Change is depicted in a lucid manner .The reader enjoys the thought processing and the way to garner hidden talent without fear to attempt any new venture. Epilogue presents the spectrum of technical terms in an unique manner. A must read for the young n old generation. Jayanta & Binita Bagchi, Asansol

HEALING POWER OF BREATHING: FIRST EDITION: LATE JUNE 2015.

- The passion and simplicity with which you have brought the subject of breathing and its power on human mind is wonderful. You shall be happy to know that few monks in RKM are interested in this book of yours. From some of my known Swamijis in eastern India, I understand your Gurudev was well known for his work...........Sri Sukhendu Bikask Misra, Founder and Managing Director, Minex India, Mumbai
- Going through "Healing power of Breathing" authored by Sri T K Pal, it is encouraging to learn the amazing power of Breathing. The author has systematically portrayed important aspects of breathing phenomenon, function, techniques to control Mind-Body complex in physical body and pranic body with reference to spirituality highlighting intimate Breath-Prana-Spirituality linkage. Presentation of facts and discussions are crisp and easy to understand for the readers to

grasp the essence, to get inspired and motivated to make the most of this inherent Divine Power in flushing negative energy and negative thought forms out of the system and attract Divine Blessing in awakening Kundalini energy to experience Divine Bliss and illumination. The fascinating idea of conveying awareness of this Great Power is significant in the present day scenario.......Sri Bidyut Kumar Ghosh. Geological survey of India, Kolkata. A devotee of Kriya Yoga.

- An excellent book not only for the beginners but also for the regular practitioners of kriya yoga. K. Jayaraman, Chennai.
- Recently I have studied a book : HEALING POWER OF BREATHING written by one of our FB friend Sri Tarit Kumar Pal & enjoyed very much. It is a very informative book which gives knowledge about benefits of proper and controlled breathing, which improves concentration, de-toxifies our body, reduces stress, improves skill to cope emotional turmoil, deepens our meditation & spiritual connection with Supreme Being, improves oxygenation & circulation of blood, increases vital energy and regulates nervous system. The book is divided into three parts. 1st part gives us awareness about the breathing phenomenon, like details of respiratory track. art of breathing, mechanism of oxygen absorption in the body, different types of breathing, Importance of deep breathing, the breath and it's influence on emotions, advantage of abdominal breathing etc.. 2nd Part gives us awareness about relationship between breath and prana, details of 5 types

of pranas & and functions, different types of nadis through which prana vayu flows, details of different chakras which control flow of prana for proper functioning of our body. 3rd Part gives us awareness about how how breath and prana governs our spiritual development, through which track we should flow our prana for self realisation and how we can reach to our SOUL with the awakening of kundalini shakti, different layers of our body, different types of pranayama, five basic elements of nature etc. I will request my friends to study the book if possible for increasing knowledge about how our body is functioning. Generally we are interested to know about the Universe but we don't want to know about " I " my body - which belongs to my SOUL.

Finally, I give my thanks to the author for writing such an informative book.

---- ----------Asit Bhattacharjee, Belur, Kolkata, a devotee of Kriya Yoga.